# California LOOK VW

## Keith Seume

*To those for whom four cylinders will always be enough.*

Published 1995 by
Bay View Books Ltd
The Red House, 25-26 Bridgeland Street
Bideford, Devon EX39 2PZ

ISBN 1 870979 63 X
Printed in Hong Kong

AUTHOR'S NOTE
All photographs in this book have been credited, where known,
to the original photographer or magazine. If this has not been possible,
then they are credited to the person from whose album they came.
To everyone who made this unique collection of photographs
of a bygone age available to me, I offer my sincere thanks.

Front Cover: Stéphane Szantai's Old School Oval.
Back Cover: EMPI's legendary *Inch Pincher Too*.

# CONTENTS

# Foreword

The expression "California Look" has been in use for over 20 years, having first been coined by freelance journalist Jere Alhadeff while writing for *Hot VWs* magazine. He wrote a feature about the fast street-legal Volkswagens that were becoming an increasingly common sight on the roads of Orange County, a suburb of Los Angeles, bringing together five examples of the "Look".

Among these was a white 1963 Beetle with a black sunroof, highly modified engine and a set of BRM magnesium wheels. That car - owned by Jim Holmes but originally built by Greg Aronson - struck a chord with Volkswagen owners across southern California and captured the true spirit of the new style perfectly. And so it should have done, for this car is now acclaimed as the first of the breed - the first California Look Volkswagen.

Today, the expression "California Look" has become part of everyday language for Volkswagen enthusiasts but all too few are aware of its origins - and that is why this book has been written. It is a tale that has been left untold for too many years.

The story begins back in the mid-1950s with the opening of a company by the name of European Motor Products Inc., or EMPI for short, and continues with the increased successes of the Volkswagen in competition. It is a story of people and their memories of an era when the Volkswagen Bug ruled the streets and strips of southern California. It is a story of clubs and camaraderie, Bug-Ins, rallies and street racing - and of a performance industry that grew up to serve a market hungry for horsepower.

But above all, it is the story of how one car grew to become the focal point of so many people's lives. No other car in history has captured the imagination of so many and no other car ever will.

Like any such book, *California Look VW* could not have been written without the help of many people, and I have listed as many as I can remember below. However, of these I must single out four people who have devoted much time and effort on my behalf, and with hand on heart I can say that I could not have done it without them.

First, my good friend Dean Kirsten has been an endless source of encouragement and information. Dean was in the thick of the California Look scene over 20 years ago and has helped me to unearth a wealth of photographs and track down an army of people to interview.

Ron Fleming - what can I say that hasn't been said before? Ron is quite probably the most enthusiastic person you could ever wish to meet. His knowledge of the early VW scene is second to none and his ability to 'persuade' others into lending a hand has to be witnessed to be appreciated!

Roger Grago provided a tremendous insight into the "middle years" of the California Look scene and made available a unique collection of memorabilia. I have never met anybody with such a photographic memory.

Finally, Bill Schwimmer, not only for coming up with so many useful contacts, but also for doing more than anyone else to keep the spirit of the original California Look alive today.

If I have one regret, it is that this - or indeed any book - is too short to be able to record everything that happened, tell every story or show every photograph. However, I hope that *California Look VW* will go some way to giving you, the reader, an insight into what makes the California Look so special.

Thank you all. Let us hope you derive as much pleasure from this book as I did from compiling it!

**Keith Seume**
Crondall, England, January 1995

The author wishes to thank the following people for their help while researching this book:

Dean Kirsten; Ron Fleming; Roger Grago; Bill Schwimmer; Greg Aronson; Jere Alhadeff; Greg & Pam Bunch; Dave Dolan; John Lazenby; Jim Edmiston; Rick Zavala; Matt Joy; Gene & Dee Berg; Dave & Judy Kawell; Dean Lowry; Darrell Vittone; Mark and Paul Schley; Rich Kimball; Dyno Don Chamberlin; Lonnie & Pam Reed; Bill Taylor; Tom Lieb; Dave Rhoades; Frenchy De Houx; Keith Goss; Ron Rosevaar; Bruce Simurda; Stéphane Szantai; Hector Bonilla; Dave Mason; Mike Key; Peter Mills (photo lab); the staff of *Hot VWs* magazine; *VolksWorld* magazine and Gwynn Thomas.

To those I have temporarily forgotten, I apologize - I have met so many people and made so many new friends that it has been quite overwhelming!

# THE PIONEERS

## A HISTORY OF THE PEOPLE AND COMPANIES THAT STARTED THE VW PERFORMANCE INDUSTRY

Since the earliest days of the aftermarket Volkswagen industry, one name has shone above all others: EMPI. No other name is shrouded in so much mystique and few other companies' products have become so collectable.

The story begins with Joe Vittone opening a Volkswagen dealership in 1954 with business partner Holt Haughey. This agency, known as Economotors, located in Riverside, was one of the earliest in California and it soon grew to be one of the most successful, selling VW Bugs and buses and service parts. Vittone soon discovered a shortcoming as far as the Volkswagen cylinder head was concerned in that the valve guides wore out at a comparatively low mileage and there were no Volkswagen-approved repair parts available. Indeed, Volkswagen's advice to repair shops was to discard entire heads and replace them with new parts.

**Joe Vittone founded the Economotors Volkswagen agency in Riverside in 1954. A little over a year later, in 1956, European Motor Products Inc (EMPI) was launched. This rare photograph shows the new building ready for business.**
(Darrell Vittone)

As a result, Vittone decided to manufacture his own valve guides, which allowed old or worn cylinder heads to be repaired and thus saved from being prematurely scrapped. These valve guides sold like hot cakes, saving Volkswagen owners countless thousands of dollars. The new venture grew to be a very profitable sideline to the Economotors dealership and so European Motor Products Inc (EMPI) was founded.

In the mid-1950s, the whole automotive performance scene started to take off, with the majority of Detroit manufacturers offering high-

The very first production BRM wheel. These wheels were made for EMPI by Graham Hill's Speedwell operation in England. Cast by Rubery Owen from 90% pure magnesium, they have become the most collectable wheels ever made. (Darrell Vittone)

Darrell Vittone preparing a 36hp engine prior to running it on the EMPI dynamometer. The photograph dates back to 1963 and shows an early equal-length exhaust system and an aftermarket carburetor set-up being used.
(Darrell Vittone)

powered versions of their regular production cars. Chevrolet started the ball rolling when it developed the new small-block V8 and slipped it into the 1955 model range. Others soon followed suit. This increasing interest in automotive performance started Joe Vittone thinking – after all, one of the most common complaints about the Volkswagen was that it was too slow.

In Germany, Okrasa was by now well established, producing performance equipment for the Volkswagen engine. In 1956 EMPI added Okrasa to its range, thus introducing the Volkswagen owner to the world of high performance. However, success wasn't instant, for Vittone recalls that "Up until the day Volkswagen introduced the 40hp engine, some owners sincerely believed that 36hp was all the power any Volkswagen would ever need". Fortunately this reluctance to accept change was not universal and soon the EMPI reputation began to grow. In 1958 Vittone added the products of the Austrian company, Denzel, to his line-up. Wolfgang Denzel's high-performance engine components were superbly engineered, with aluminium conrods and well-designed dual-port cylinder heads. They were more expensive than the Okrasa conversions, but of much higher quality.

In 1958 Vittone addressed the uninspiring handling characteristics of the Bug by designing a front anti-sway bar. EMPI promotional material extolled the virtues of this simple accessory – by now, just about every other motor manufacturer had equipped their cars with anti-sway bars as a matter of course – stating that the car would no longer lean so much in corners or be affected by side-winds to such a large degree. Again, there was scepticism from some quarters, but that was soon dispelled when in 1959 Volkswagen made an anti-sway bar a stock

**Of the many combinations tried by EMPI over the years, the Shorrocks supercharger proved to be one of the most successful.**

**Developed in association with Chris Shorrocks in England, the units were purchased from Sidney Allard.**
(Dean Lowry)

fitment on the Bug. Indeed, the Karmann Ghia range had been fitted with anti-sway bars from the very beginning.

Following the success of the anti-sway bar, Vittone designed a rear stabiliser that addressed the problem of wheels tucking under during hard cornering. This was a characteristic of cars with swing-axle suspension and severely limited the handling potential of all early Porsches and VWs. The stabiliser bar, or camber compensator as it became known, was put to good use on the 1956 VW sedan (later to achieve fame as the *Inch Pincher* drag racer) which Dan Gurney drove in the 1963 Grand Prix of Volkswagens in Nassau. It proved to be a huge success and ultimately over 100,000 were sold worldwide.

By this time the name of the company had been changed to Engineered Motor Products Incorporated, as Vittone felt that it suggested a greater emphasis on product development, and

hence quality. On one of his trips to Europe, Vittone met with Graham Hill, world champion racing driver and future winner of the Indianapolis 500. Hill's company, Speedwell, manufactured a range of components for British and European cars which proved to be of interest to the EMPI boss. Discussions led to Speedwell being granted the manufacturing rights to some of the EMPI Volkswagen parts, including the camber compensator. In return, Speedwell began development of some purely VW-related equipment which EMPI then added to its product range.

In 1963 Joe and Darrell Vittone visited Speedwell's headquarters at Chesham in England, leaving behind a Volkswagen on which to develop the prototype dual-Stromberg carburetor kit. Talks were also held on that trip with Tony Rudd, head of BRM (for whom Graham Hill had been driving in Grand Prix events), with regard to the design and manufacture of the famous BRM magnesium wheel, and with Chris Shorrock, manufacturer of the Shorrocks supercharger kits. These kits were later purchased through Sidney Allard, who had world distribution rights for Shorrocks superchargers.

**Fontana Raceway, April 3rd 1966. Dean Lowry (right) poses with the *Inch Pincher* race car, a pair of EMPI demonstrator cars and the company pick-up. One of EMPI's greatest strengths was always its excellent presentation at all times.** (Dean Lowry)

**A proud Lowry looks out from behind the wheel of the *Inch Pincher*. Note how the name has now changed from European to Engineered Motor Products. Note, too, the unusual variation of the BRM wheel with different spokes.**
(Dean Lowry)

With much of the product development being carried out by EMPI employee Dean Lowry on the *Inch Pincher* race car, the company soon established a reputation for producing a range of high-quality performance parts for the VW. In reality, the greater part of the EMPI catalogue was taken up with dress-up parts but there was no denying that certain of the performance parts, such as the high-ratio rocker arms, 88mm slipper-skirt pistons and cylinders, the extensive range of carburetor kits and the wheels, were the very best available.

EMPI's greatest strength was always its marketing. Handled entirely in-house, the production of catalogs, posters and clothing served to promote the EMPI name in all four corners of the automotive world. Heinz Jung was the person responsible for much of the photography and decal design. His classic "Sorry 'bout that!" decal became a familiar sight affixed to the back window of EMPI-tuned VWs, apologizing to the owners of much larger cars for out-performing them on the street and strip.

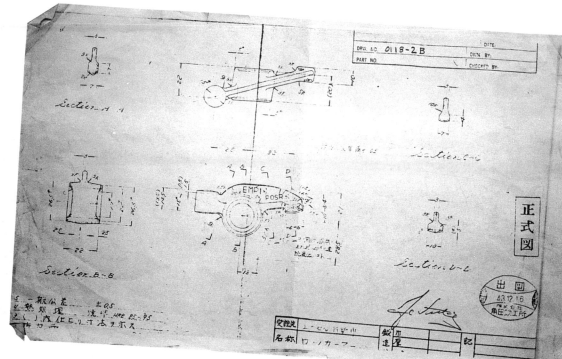

Some of the finest products manufactured by EMPI were its high-ratio rocker arm assemblies. These came to be the standard fitment on just about every drag race or fast street Volkswagen throughout the late 1960s and '70s. (Author)

EMPI was the master of marketing, with a whole range of clothing, decals, catalogs and other promotional material being made available to customers and agents alike. Articles such as the EMPI jacket are highly collectable today. (Author)

EMPI was one of the few companies to launch its own newspaper for distribution to its dealers. Called *The Accelerator*, it detailed all the latest products including, as shown here, the GTV Beetle, EMPI's own sporty Bug. (Author)

Owning a VW agency and the EMPI operation, Vittone was in a unique position. In 1966 he was able to offer complete new cars that carried a range of EMPI parts yet remained covered by a full warranty. These cars, known as the EMPI GTVs, were available in four levels of equipment. The MkI was a VW 1300 with the addition of a complete set of dress-up parts, front anti-sway bar, camber compensator, E-Z-R gear shift, sports exhaust system and a set of chrome wheels. GTV emblems on the quarter panels completed the package. The

**EMPI recognized the growing interest in the dune buggy and manufactured the EMPI Imp to take advantage of this expanding market. The example shown here is fitted with a pair of Sprint Star wheels and Speedwell bucket seats.** (Darrell Vittone)

**The *Jouster* was EMPI's ill-fated attempt at building a record-setting drag race car. The glassfiber-bodied vehicle was powered by a supercharged VW engine running through a Porsche transmission. Car was eventually crashed at OCIR.** (Dean Lowry)

MkI kit cost $437.20 over and above the price of a stock 1300 Bug.

The MkII added a number of other dress-up parts to the MkI's specification, including a rear parcel shelf complete with additional speakers, engine lid lock and dual back-up lights. The cost of this package was $566.85. The MkIII added some extra instrumentation, some more dress-up parts and, best of all, a set of BRM wheels. The cost of all this was just $755.05. Finally, the MkIV package included all of the above, plus a ram-induction carburetor kit, brake servo, seat recliners and a set of Boge shock absorbers. The GTV MkIV kit retailed for $1238.75 complete.

The EMPI empire expanded across the USA, with no fewer than 28 distributors and an incredible 489 agents spread throughout 43 states. Many of these agents were also Volkswagen dealerships and that fact did not please Volkswagen

of America at all. Its representatives applied a lot of pressure in an effort to get these agencies to sever their ties with EMPI, even going so far as to cut their quotas of new cars at a time when there was already a shortage of new models. As Darrell Vittone says, it's too bad that Volkswagen wasn't smart enough to appreciate the youth market back then like his father did.

In 1971 the EMPI story began to draw to a close with its sale to Filter Dynamics, manufacturers of Lee automotive filters. The sale came about largely because Vittone wished to devote more of his time to Economotors and the saddest part of the tale is that the deal involved him being paid in stock which ultimately "went down the toilet", to quote son Darrell. As a consequence, Vittone ended up with virtually nothing from the deal. (Incidentally, Revmaster, another long-established VW specialist company, was another victim of Filter Dynamics.) At

The tiny EMPI dragster was one of a number of VW-powered rails campaigned in the early 1960s. Lee Leighton, the driver, looks a little bashful in this photograph, taken at Bug-In 1 on October 20th 1968 at OCIR. (Darrell Vittone)

Dean Lowry adds some oil to the dashpot of one of the two Stromberg carburetors used in EMPI's Sprint kit. Lowry carried out much of the development work while he was employed by EMPI, before eventually leaving to start DDS. (Dean Lowry)

its peak EMPI sold up to $6 million worth of parts a year (maybe as much as ten times that at today's prices), a figure unlikely ever to be repeated.

Darrell Vittone left EMPI in 1972 to open The Race Shop with partners Dave Andrews and cylinder head wizard Fumio Fukaya. Gradually the EMPI empire went into decline until its demise in 1974. The problem was that Filter Dynamics, being a large corporate operation, did not have that hands-on experience of the VW market to make it pay. Ultimately, the name was sold again and now graces a range of dress-up parts sold under the EMPI-Mr Bug name.

Dean Lowry began his relationship with Volkswagens when he joined Economotors in 1955. One of his first tasks was to pull the engine out of a Bug and replace the clutch. When he saw how easy it was to work on the motor once it was on the work bench, he decided that Volkswagens were for him! Lowry left after a while and, following a couple of other jobs, ended up working for Century Motors, the Volkswagen agency in Alhambra.

While there, he helped to prepare and race a VW at the old San Gabriel drag strip. After four or five months, a representative of Volkswagen came along and told Century Motors that they couldn't do separate advertising! The guy standing next to the VW man, who happened to be from Porsche, spoke up and said, "We don't care about that sort of thing. If you stick a Porsche motor in it, that's OK by us!" So Lowry built a Porsche-engined dragster which he campaigned in numerous local events.

After another few months, Joe Vittone asked Dean to join him again, which he did in 1963,

Soon after EMPI was sold to Filter Dynamics, Darrell Vittone (left) formed the Race Shop with Dave Andrews and Fumio Fukaya. With a new business came a new race car and continuing success on the strip. Jim Bentley on the right.
(Darrell Vittone)

Following the departure of Lowry, Joe Vittone's son, Darrell, took over the *Inch Pincher* driving chores. The car was steadily revamped with a whole new look, but its winning ways continued, helping further establish the EMPI name.
(Darrell Vittone)

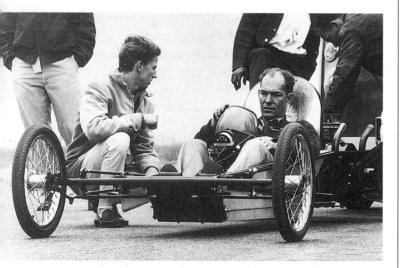

Fontana Raceway, 1966. Lowry prepares to make a pass in the tiny original EMPI dragster. Note the side-winder engine configuration: single-speed chain drive was used. Lowry understandably looks a little apprehensive.
(Dean Lowry)

working as part of the EMPI operation. His involvement included the development of exhaust systems, carburetor kits and valve gear, as well as building the original *Inch Pincher*. This car became the center of his attention for the next five years.

During that period Lowry came to be respected as quite possibly the greatest of all Volkswagen drag racers, with numerous victories at the wheel of this, the most famous of all race cars. For example, in 1965, the first year in which *Inch Pincher* was campaigned, Lowry shared the driving with Darrell Vittone. In their first season they won three out of seven divisional meetings, six out of seven NHRA events and reset the national record each time out. They capped that first season by winning the overall points series. An auspicious debut by anybody's reckoning.

In 1968 Dean Lowry and his brother Ken decided to set up business by themselves in Santa Ana. Part of the reason for Lowry leaving EMPI was

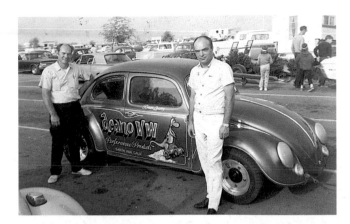

The Brothers Lowry -
Dean on the left, Ken on
the right - stand proudly
alongside their famous
purple race car. The color
dominated the DDS
empire with everything,
including the building,
succumbing to a coat of
purple paint!
(Dean Lowry)

**Lowry loved racing the
big boys most of all and
his days spent in NHRA
competition were the
most enjoyable.
Irwindale Raceway saw
plenty of action over the
years, including the ever-
popular night racing.**
(Dean Lowry)

that he wished to work on engines full time; at EMPI there were so many other things going on that wasn't always possible. The first shop was an 1,800sq ft unit which they moved into in August that year. By the following April the Lowry brothers had run out of space so moved into a larger, 6,000sq ft building on East Borchard, Santa Ana, and expanded from there. Sadly, the relationship between Joe Vittone and Dean Lowry broke down as a result of the brothers going it alone.

The new business was called Deano Dyno-Soars Inc. Dean's nickname while he was at EMPI was Deano Dyno (Vittone used to call him Dino, or Deano) as a result of the hours Lowry used to spend on the shop dynamometer. Ken Lowry said, "The kids saw the Hanna-Barbera cartoon *The Flintstones* and started calling Dean 'Deano' after the Neanderthal housepet of Fred and Wilma", and so the name well and truly stuck. The prehistoric connection led to "dinosaur" becoming corrupted to "Dyno-Soar" in honour of all that dyno time at EMPI. DDS even adopted the cartoon of Hanna-Barbera's creation as a shop mascot, incorporating it into the logo and eventually painting it on the shop race car. The dinosaur theme was expanded still further when the brothers started to market big-bore conversion kits for the 40hp VW engine. The kit was called the "Brawn-to-Soarus"....

The Lowrys had learnt a lot about marketing from EMPI and, following the prehistoric theme, became infatuated with the color purple. This began after they took note of two of the best-known engine builders in mainstream drag racing: Ed Pink and Keith Black. Pink and Black worked primarily on Chrysler Hemi engines, nicknamed "Elephant" motors because of their sheer size. The prospect of "Pink Elephants" amused the Lowrys and so they came up with the Purple Dyno-Soar engine. Not only were the engines painted purple but so were the race car and the entire DDS building!

**Wheelstanding action from the *Dyno-Soar*. Dean Lowry was always a very relaxed driver, even when things got out of control! DDS logo upset Hanna-Barbera, owners of the Flintstones TV series, due to its similarity to Fred's pet dinosaur.**
(NHRA)

**The crowning glory for DDS was the design and production of the aftermarket crankcase and cylinder heads. The 'case allowed cranks with a very long stroke to be used, while the heads flowed better than any modified Volkswagen part.**
(Dean Lowry)

When the Lowrys decided to go racing, they used Dean's daily street car as the basis. It was a 1954 VW sedan which was extensively lightened. It ran a 2180cc engine and became a front-running car in NHRA H/Gas racing, running regularly down into the mid-eleven second bracket. Lowry campaigned the car with considerable success until 1972, when he decided to sell out. "Too many miles and too much time" was the reason for the sale; competing in the NHRA series across the United States for several years in succession had taken its toll. During this period, the Lowrys helped many other racers with their cars, including the Schley brothers (who were in fact the first people to be taken on as DDS employees - Gene Berg was to work there later, too) in *Lightning Bug* and Audley Campbell in *Stutt Bee*.

The business closed in 1972 and the Brothers Lowry, as they were always called, went their separate ways. Ken started his own business, ARPM, while Dean moved to Tucson, Arizona, until 1982. He then moved back to Santa Ana where he carried

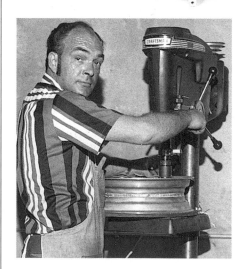

**Ken Lowry adds the finishing touches to a batch of DDS lightweight spun-aluminum wheels. These were among the first wheels designed specifically for use on drag race VWs, although some sets did make an appearance on streetcars.**
(Dean Lowry)

out a lot of research work on Mazda and Toyota motors, as well as continuing development of VW parts, for a further nine years. He then moved back out to Glendale, Arizona where he currently resides.

During their period together, the Brothers Lowry developed a number of interesting components under the DDS name including, in 1983, one of the first sets of aftermarket cylinder heads for the Volkswagen drag racer. These heads featured oval Cosworth-style inlet ports and more material round the combustion chamber that allowed larger valves to be fitted than would be possible in a welded VW head.

The crowning glory of their development work, though, had to be the Ultra Case - an aftermarket crankcase for Volkswagen engines that enabled engines of up to 3 litres to be built. The brothers also developed their own line of lightweight racing wheels which became the chosen fitment of many drag racers in the 1970s - they would also make their appearance on at least one of the first California Look sedans to hit the street.

Having been involved with Volkswagens for almost 40 years, Gene Berg's name is synonymous with VW high performance. His company, Gene Berg Enterprises in Orange, is generally acknowledged as manufacturer of some of the finest VW parts around.

His first introduction to the marque was through his uncle back in the mid-1950s when he was living

**A young Gene Berg poses alongside his first Volkswagen - a black 1956 sedan bought new from a VW agency in Washington. The car proved to be rather slow after the V8-powered '40 Ford that Berg had been used to driving.**
(Gene Berg)

in Washington State. Impressed by what he saw, the young Berg ordered a new black 1956 sedan which he enjoyed driving but found rather slow after his old '40 Ford with its V8 flathead motor. A friend owned a machine shop, where the carburetor venturi was bored out, distributor recurved and the compression ratio raised slightly. Other people saw what he had done and asked him to work on their cars, too. The '56 made way for a '60 which was bought new in 1960.

In October that year, he got himself a job at a Volkswagen dealership in Renton, Washington and, the following year, the '60 made way for an ex-demo 1961 Bug. Berg began to work on the 40hp engine, adding a set of Porsche cylinders with Ford flathead pistons, and then bought some Okrasa parts from EMPI, including a pair of dual-port heads. Soon after, he added one of Okrasa's stroker crankshafts.

By 1962 he was helping a friend, Lanny Lawrence, who had a built a dragster called *Little But Quick* which ran a Porsche industrial engine with a stock Zenith carburetor. When Lawrence decided to move out of the area, Berg bought the dragster. In 1963 he slipped a 74mm stroker crank into a VW engine and modified some Chevrolet Corvair cylinders and 3¾ins oversized forged pistons to fit, resulting in a capacity of 115ci (1884cc). With modified Okrasa heads, home-made manifolds and dual Solex 40P11 carburetors, the little dragster ran well down into the eleven second bracket, recording a best of 11.19secs.

Berg sold the dragster, less engine, and retired from racing for about a year until some friends

invited him along to a meeting. He decided he might as well slip the engine into his sedan and see what happened. The end result was a car that ran quicker than Dean Lowry in EMPI's *Inch Pincher* - Berg ran a best of 13.80 secs with that combination at a time when Lowry held the H/Gas record with a 14.30. The next step was to fit a pair of the new VW dual-port cylinder heads when they became available and buy a pair of manifolds from EMPI. As these soon broke, Berg cast up his own and so gradually began to manufacture parts from scratch.

The first of these, the deep sump, was to become something of a Berg trademark and was soon followed by close-ratio gear sets for VW transmissions. At the time, just about everybody who raced a Volkswagen had been forced to switch over to Porsche transmissions in order to take advantage of the better ratios. When Berg came down to California to compete in a drag race, he was offered the chance to drive Lowry's car and sample close-ratio gears for the first time. He promptly went home and made his own using a drill-press and hand files. In Berg's own words, they were "simply awful" but they got the job done.

Dual 48IDA Weber carburetors were the next logical development and Berg recalls buying them from Carroll Shelby late in 1966 for just $36 a piece - and rues the day he didn't buy a whole warehouse-full at that price!

At the time there were no slicks made to fit a Volkswagen so, like everybody else, Berg used Casler recapped racing tyres on his Bug. On one trip to the Winternationals at Pomona, the superior traction offered by the well-prepared track caused an undue

Gene Berg and Jim Sibley (in crash helmet) with Lanny Lawrence's Porsche-powered dragster. Little rail was basic in the extreme, but eventually ran down into the very low elevens. Compare the size with the domestic sedan behind! (Gene Berg)

The dragster, nicknamed *Little But Quick*, relied on a Porsche industrial engine (as shown here) equipped with a single Zenith carburetor. When Berg bought the machine in 1963 he slipped in an 1884cc VW-based engine with dual Solexes. (Gene Berg)

amount of wheel hop off the starting line. This broke the transmission nose-cone and allowed the engine to move freely. Towing the car afterwards on an A-frame behind his VW bus proved to be an interesting experience, as the broken gearbox mounting allowed the rear wheels of the Bug to move around at will. Once back home, Berg figured out how to cure the problem and fabricated a simple bar that passed under the back of the engine and located to the stock bumper mounts with a pair of turnbuckles. This cured the problem instantly, becoming the forerunner of the traction bar used on almost every high-performance VW today.

In 1968, when the Brothers Lowry decided to set up in business by themselves, Berg manufactured various parts for their company, including carburetor linkages, manifolds, sumps and close-ratio gears. He took the plunge and moved down from Washington in 1969 to join them for a while. However, a difference of opinion with Ken Lowry saw Berg move out and into some space in "Dirty" Dave Vanderbeke's shop for a month. He then rented his own premises in Orange, opening up shop on December 15th 1969 in Lemon St, Orange. Later, in 1975, he would move to the current address on Lime. Who else can claim to have moved from Lemon to Lime and stayed in Orange?

Over the next few years, he concentrated on developing new products, one of the best known being counterweighted crankshafts for VWs, which were designed in conjunction with Bob Dixon. High-ratio rocker arms are a common bolt-on

**Not many people would want to try this trick. Gary Berg had the opportunity to drive the Tayco *Madness* car as well as the family race car at the same NHRA meeting, resulting in speedy legwork swapping between the cars after each round!**
(Jere Alhadeff)

**Few people have got as much fun out of working on Volkswagens as Berg. Here he steps behind the wheel of son Gary's street car prior to taking a trip down the quarter mile at Orange County. Note the flower-power interior trim!**
(Jere Alhadeff)

performance modification today, but back in the mid- to late-'60s they were something new. The first set Berg made came about after he had Sig Erson grind a race camshaft for the '64 sedan he then owned. Once fitted, Berg noticed an improvement, but felt that there was room for more, so contacted Erson once again.

The cam grinder was amazed that the little VW motor could handle the amount of valve lift and duration offered by the camshaft, casually asking what ratio rocker arms Berg was using. The reply

was stock, 1:1. That was the reason for the lack of power: Erson's race cam was designed to be used with a 1.4 or 1.5:1 ratio rocker. Berg went into the workshop and welded up a set of rocker arms using, first of all, some rockers off an Austrian Glas and then others using intake rocker arms from a Porsche 356. These were to become the prototypes for the original high-lift rocker assemblies.

A lot of development work went into producing large-bore pistons and cylinders for Volkswagens over the years, the industry standard always having been EMPI's superb 88mm slipper-skirt pistons in the Biral aluminium barrels. In 1970 Berg worked with Mahle to produce the first 90.5mm (1776cc with a stock crank) using a 3⁹⁄₁₆in Corvair piston. Earlier, in 1969, NPR had used a 3⅝in Dodge piston to make the 92mm (1835cc) conversion. As time passed, Berg experimented with many different combinations of parts, some readily available, others manufactured in-house to his own design. Among the best-known of his products are the dual carburetor linkages, gear shifters, exhaust systems and crankshafts, all having an unparalleled reputation for quality.

Although Berg has raced many different vehicles, by far the best-known is the family's black '67 sedan. This was purchased as a stolen car which had been recovered but found partially stripped. It had no interior, decklid, fenders, etc., but Berg bought, sold and swapped until he had accumulated all the correct parts to rebuild the sedan. At first his wife

**In the 1990s the Berg sedan continues its winning ways, running a best time of 10.39secs/127.27mph. The trademark BRMs remain** on the front, but have had to give way to some aluminum rims at the back to allow the fitment of wider slicks. (Author)

Dee drove it but after a while it was fitted with the engine from Don Ruckman's *Sonic Muffin* race car and driven by Don in a few races. It wasn't long before an engine was built for the car and the driving chores taken over by Berg's son Gary.

The car has grown to be part of Volkswagen folklore, almost certainly being the most successful – and most definitely the longest lasting – VW race vehicle in history. What started out as a stock street car became a regular winner in A/MC in NHRA competition and a force to be reckoned with at the Bug-Ins. Almost 20 years later, the '67 was to take the Super Street record in PRA (Professional Racing Association) classes in the early 1990s, running a best time of 10.39secs/127.27mph. No other car can claim that kind of heritage. With the black sedan acting as a rolling test-bed for new products, if ever proof was needed of how racing improves the breed, then this is it.

The Berg family continues to compete (sons Doug and Clyde each race their own sedans) with a

**Berg can always be relied upon to act the clown when the opportunity arises - something tells us he would look more at ease behind the wheel of the race car rather than testing a skateboard in this 1975 photograph but, nothing ventured...** (Gene Berg)

One of the simplest yet most effective logos ever designed was the side-on view of the 48IDA Weber used by Fleming, Aronson & Thurber Performance (otherwise known simply as FAT Performance). Logo was dreamt up by Ron Fleming. (Ron Fleming)

FAT Performance has always carried out the majority of machine work in-house, allowing greater scope to experiment with new ideas. Ron Fleming operates the Bridgeport mill while machining a Porsche 911 cylinder head. (Ron Fleming)

great deal of success, their trademark BRM wheels being the envy of many a race fan.

One company whose name is synonymous with VW high-performance and the growth of the California Look is FAT Performance. Ron Fleming began his working life at a repair shop called Westphalia Motors. After a short while he left to join S&S Racing over in Orange, a small import repair business which was trying to establish a VW performance center. At the time, around 1969, Gene Berg was working at Deano Dyno-Soars in Santa Ana, but soon left to start on his own. Fleming and Berg became good friends so Fleming left S&S to join Berg's new company. He started out as the counter salesman, handling all the day-to-day business that came into the shop.

Berg taught Fleming a lot about VW engines but, by the same token, Fleming taught Berg a lot in

return. He handled the production of most of Berg's product releases, something for which the company became famous in later years. In the meantime Fleming had become pretty adept at engine building and earned himself a good reputation with other members of his club, Der Kleiner Panzers. Fellow club member Greg Aronson was in need of a job and, as his specialty at that time was building VW transmissions, he was offered a position at Gene Berg's in the summer of 1969.

This arrangement lasted for a few months before Greg decided to leave and go it alone. To begin with he worked out of the family garage, where he had to set up shop when his father drove to work in the morning and break everything down again when he returned in the evening. The workbenches were designed to fold away against the walls to make things easier. Soon after, Ron Fleming left Berg's to join Greg in business. The two had a great life,

**Ron Fleming (standing), Greg Aronson (right) and Mark Thurber (left) - the 'F', 'A' and 'T' of FAT respectively. The trio are posed next to Aronson's** **innovative 1963 ragtop sedan, acknowledged as being the first of the California Look cars.** (Ron Fleming)

working just three days a week and heading for the beach the rest of the time. Weekends were reserved for drag racing, though. With no responsibilities such as wives or children, Fleming and Aronson were more than happy with the situation.

Unfortunately for them, neither the police nor Aronson's father shared their enthusiasm. Greg's dad hadn't minded when his son was just working on his own, but felt that setting up a business with a partner was stretching the goodwill a little too far. Police, for their part, complained regularly about customers' cars sitting out on the street, minus their engines. The suggestion from all parties was that it was time for the partners to go and find some proper premises.

To start with, in July 1971, they rented a shop in an industrial park behind Anaheim stadium. Their plan was to work three days a week and enjoy themselves for the remaining four. Somehow that

idea didn't quite work out, and soon they were working a full six days a week. When they moved in they had just two months' rent, $500-worth of parts, their two tool boxes and engine stands. They built work benches in the 1,000sq ft workshop and, once word got round, never looked back. Soon they had outgrown their work space and rented another unit that offered 5,000sq ft. Another move saw them rent an even larger building in Anaheim, which they used for a further twelve years.

The original partnership expanded in 1976 when Mark Thurber was taken on board. He was left in charge of things while Fleming and Aronson headed down to Mexico with *Tar Babe*, the VW sedan raced under the company banner, but eventually it was decided that the business wasn't really large enough to bear a three-way split and Thurber left. However the company name, which began life as Fleming & Aronson VW High Performance and then grew into Fleming, Aronson & Thurber (FAT), remained FAT Performance.

Finally, in 1988 they moved to their current address in Orange. Their product range expanded

**Greg Aronson (left) helps Darrell Vittone with his new Fiat Spyder race car. Its ultra-low stance can be appreciated here in this photograph. Note the top of the 48IDA carburetor poking up above the level of the dashboard (center left).**
(Ron Fleming)

**The FAT dynamometer saw plenty of action throughout the 1970s as the company's reputation spread. Greg Aronson makes an adjustment prior to running up a 48IDA-equipped motor. A BRM wheel was used to keep the water hose tidy.**
(Ron Fleming)

steadily, covering everything from hard-core performance parts to the trademark aluminum T-bars that were designed by them to bypass the no-bumper laws of the early '70s.

Over the years the reputation of the company has grown dramatically, especially in off-road racing circles where customers' cars have competed with considerable success. However, as far as proponents of the California Look scene are concerned, FAT will be remembered for being the driving force behind the fastest street-legal VWs of the 1970s.

Another name which has been at the forefront of the Volkswagen performance industry is Scat, founded by Tom Lieb. In the late 1950s and early 1960s, to help finance his time at college, he became what was known as a core dealer. He would buy used engine parts and sell them to engine rebuilders. His involvement with Volkswagens came about by chance, when one of the companies he dealt with asked if he could supply some VW engines as it wanted to set up a rebuilding program.

About three weeks later, Lieb was in a scrapyard at the same time as somebody who was dumping a whole load of parts labelled "Volkswagen". These parts turned out to be all the warranty returns from the western region of the United States. Any part which was returned under warranty would be dispatched to Volkswagen's offices at Culver City, a suburb of Los Angeles, where they were analysed and then scrapped. Just through pure chance, Tom Lieb ran into the one person responsible for getting rid of the warranty parts.

Lieb was able to purchase new cylinder heads, crankcases and crankshafts; in fact he was able to obtain parts for the 1500cc engine even before many of the dealers held any stock. When he got out of college he turned to his new found interest full-time. He realised that there was no point in working for somebody else when he could earn more money working for himself. His first major deal was with Revmaster, one of the first Volkswagen-only engine rebuilders in the USA. He supplied them all of their core parts. Lieb's motto was "Buy low, sell high" so he went to the scrapyards and gradually began supplying rebuilders all over the west coast, including Revmaster, Scandia (who held the Montgomery Ward contract) and Engine Parts (Sears and Roebuck).

**Mark Thurber ran his own street car, too. The metallic brown sedan (photographed in 1972) was equipped with a set of BRM wheels and a hot Weber-carbed engine. A lack of chrome trim and the racing-style mirror were classic features of the new Look.** (Ron Fleming)

To begin with the business had no name. While Tom Lieb was still at college, another of his sidelines was rebuilding wrecked cars, predominantly Corvettes, with a neighborhood friend. One night, they sat around drinking Coke when his friend, not known for his optimistic outlook on life, raised the fact that one day they would have to start paying taxes, form a company, give it a name, like Scat or something, become legitimate, etc., etc.

A year or so later, in 1963 or '64, Tom Lieb

**Lieb began his working life as a core dealer, supplying engines and components to rebuilders on the west coast. Among his first major clients was one who asked Lieb to find some Volkswagen engines. His motto was "Buy low, sell high".** (Tom Lieb)

**Although he had been in business for some while, Tom Lieb finally put a name to his operation - Scat Enterprises - in '63 or '64 . Located in Inglewood, close to Los Angeles airport, Scat offered speed equipment, transmissions and machining.** (Tom Lieb)

found he really did have to get things on a legal footing. He went to the Board of Equalization to register the business, filled out all the forms, handed over his $3 and went to walk away. The clerk at the counter called him back, telling him that he hadn't completed the paperwork correctly: he hadn't written in a company name. So Lieb thought quickly and, recalling the conversation in his garage a year or two earlier said "Scat". "Is that with one 'T' or two?" came the reply. "One" said Lieb and that was that. The name Scat means nothing at all and is not, as many suggest, an acronym for Southern California Auto Tuning, or whatever.

Lieb became more aware of the growing interest in automotive performance and in 1964 opened his own speed shop in Inglewood, becoming an EMPI

distributor. He was impressed by Joe Vittone's operation and the fact that, as a VW dealer himself, he was able to sell into other VW agencies. Lieb was the one of the few non-VW agencies that EMPI sold to in any quantity at the time.

A machine shop was developed alongside the speed shop which carried out all the engine machining for Carroll Shelby (the man responsible for the Cobras and GT350 and GT500 Mustangs) who had his own workshop close by. One of Scat's first employees was Bill Taylor, who worked with Lieb until 1967 when he quit to start his own business, Tayco.

Scat published its own catalog in 1962 and concentrated on selling parts that no one else carried. It made the first ram induction manifolds for what became known as the Holley Bugspray – in fact a Holley carburetor modified from one originally fitted to a Ford truck. The young entrepreneur entered into a deal with Holley carburetors that gave him exclusive rights to the Bugspray for several years. Lieb lays claim to being the first person to fit dual 48IDA Webers to a Volkswagen engine, thanks to his contacts with Shelby. His was also the first company to explore the use of Zenith 32NDIX carburetors on the VW

In common with EMPI, Scat has always had an enviable reputation for quality packaging and promotion. Over the years Scat's marketing program has earned the company numerous design awards for product marketing.
(Tom Lieb)

The Scat of the 1990s is a far cry from the little speed shop in Inglewood of thirty years earlier. Amongst the machine work carried out by Scat is the manufacture of crankshafts for many of the leading Indy Car teams, as well as Porsche.
(Tom Lieb)

engine, sourcing the parts from French Simcas which used a version of the old Ford V8-60 flathead motor.

Scat's first crankshafts were marketed in 1966 when a crankshaft grinder was purchased. Scat reworked both regular Volkswagen and Okrasa crankshafts, to produce the first ever counterweighted stroker cranks for VWs. In 1970 the company cast its first crankshaft, expanding into a new building to cater for the increased business.

New aftermarket conrods were also manufactured from stainless steel, along with heavy duty gland nuts to secure the flywheel. In 1975 Scat cast the first aftermarket crankcase for an aircraft company, ultimately building some 3,500 *water*-cooled engines for the client. The 'case would eventually become a common sight at the VW drag races as engine builders sought something stronger and more sophisticated than the stock VW casting.

In 1971 Scat designed the flanged crankshaft to

Ever the innovator, Tom Lieb tried various intriguing combinations in the search for horsepower, including this twin-supercharged VW Type 3 engine which relied on a pair of Paxton blowers. Unfortunately it was not a great success. (Tom Lieb)

Scat enjoyed a long association with Bill Mitchell of Motion Performance on the east coast, whose *Thunder Bug* racecar was always a center of controversy. No one on the west coast ever quite believed the times recorded by the car! (Hot VWs)

help prevent the problem of the flywheel coming loose when a drag racer dropped the clutch on the start line. That same year, Tom Lieb hooked up with Bill Mitchell of Motion Minicar on the east coast, beginning a long-standing relationship that saw several national records being broken in both NHRA and IHRA competition by Mitchell's controversial *Thunderbug* race cars. In 1975 Lieb realized that the cast crankshaft was at the end of its days as far as drag racing was concerned, so he produced his first forged crankshaft for the VW engine, a component still in production today.

In common with EMPI, one of Scat's greatest strengths was – and still is – excellent packaging. All design and production was carried out in-house from day one, and over the years Scat has won many awards for packaging design. The company has remained at the forefront of the Volkswagen industry for over 30 years and today has an excellent reputation for producing extremely high quality components, especially crankshafts. Indeed, many of the world's motor manufacturers look to Scat for their prototype cranks, as do the majority of the Indy Car teams. Even Porsche has Scat manufacture all its replacement 356 and 912 crankshafts.

The Volkswagen industry has come a long way since those early days when Joe Vittone made his first valve guides or Gene Berg cast his first deep sump. Today it is a multi-million dollar industry with openings all over the world and, every year, new components are being designed and produced. Long may that remain the case.

# THE CALIFORNIA LOOK

## TRACING THE DEVELOPMENT OF THE STYLE
## FROM THE MID-1960S ONWARDS

Until the February 1975 issue of *Hot VWs* magazine was published, what has become known as the California Look had not been publicly acknowledged as a style all of its own. Twenty years later, the expression is used to describe virtually any air-cooled VW that has been lowered or otherwise customized.

It was automotive photographer Jere Alhadeff who first coined the expression California Look when he wrote an article for *Hot VWs* about the new breed of customized VW that was making an appearance on the streets of southern California. In reality, as was noted at the time, the correct terminology should have been "SoCal Look" or "Orange County Look", but who outside southern California knew where Orange County was?

Alhadeff took note of the increasing number of Volkswagens that shunned the popular trend of wide

**Greg Bunch chose to fit chrome wheels which were made up using Chevrolet rims on VW centers, with Porsche "nipple" hubcaps. Rear tires are Goodyear Blue Streaks. Pat at Anchor Headers made the one-off exhaust system.** (Greg Bunch)

**The first time the California Look received public recognition was when Jim Holmes' car made the front cover of the February 1975 issue of *Hot VWs* magazine - over five years after it had been built by Greg Aronson.** (Author)

fenders, mag wheels and metallic paint by appearing to mimic the drag race cars of heroes such as Dean Lowry, Darrell Vittone and the Schley Brothers. This growing band of fast street VWs placed a greater emphasis on slippery looks, tasteful paint and a lot of horsepower.

Although the late Jim Wright, then publisher of *Hot VWs*, reluctantly acknowledged that there were such VWs running round the streets of Costa Mesa, Anaheim and neighboring areas, he felt that the style was too subtle to be appreciated by the magazine's readers. Wright believed that no one outside the immediate area would be interested in such a look. As a consequence, Alhadeff was persuaded to include at least one vehicle which was far too "custom" to be considered part of the Look, Mike Lemire's flamed and chromed '56 show car. Its inclusion was for the sake of those readers who could not appreciate the finer points of the true California Look. The Karmann Ghia coupé of Roger Grago was also included, to show that the new style could be applied to cars other than just Bugs. However, at the time there were very few people actually working on Ghias.

Part of the reason for this is that the Karmann Ghia was a rare sight on the drag strip. Dave Kawell was almost certainly the first to drag race a Ghia, disproving a certain person in the industry's theories that the weight distribution and aerodynamics were all wrong for drag racing by building a pair of very successful cars. However, even when the Ghia did gain a greater acceptance on the strip, California Look versions would always be thin on the ground.

It is important not get the impression that the classic California Look happened overnight with one magazine feature. Prior to its recognition, a lengthy period of evolution took place, beginning with the cars of the original members of Volkswagens Limited, forerunner of the famed Der Kleiner Panzers VW Club (DKP). These pioneers developed a club style all of its own which instantly set their cars apart from those of other VW clubs. Back in these early days – 1965-66 – their cars were almost exclusively Volkswagen Bugs although, as the style developed, Karmann Ghias, Type 2s (buses) and the occasional Type 3 (Squareback) did begin to make an appearance on the scene. One body style that never really formed a part of the original DKP California Look was the convertible Bug, for the simple reason that no one really raced a convertible. . . ..

The favored club style was simple at first. In common with later examples of the California Look, the early DKP cars tended to reflect the state of the art drag race VWs and that meant that wide fenders and fat tires were out. One of the most common modifications was to fit a pair of Porsche 356 steel rims to the rear of the car, sometimes chromed, often painted silver, on which Goodyear Blue Streak tires were mounted. Although these tires did not offer a great deal of grip in the wet, they hooked up hard in dry conditions. They also looked very cool with their Goodyear Sports Car Special lettering and slim blue line round the sidewall. In

**Mike Joseph's '65 shows off its chrome Porsche 356 wheels and radial tires. Porsche hubcaps are used only at the front, while at the rear the brake drums have been painted. Anchor Headers logo on rear fender was common.**
(Greg Bunch)

some cases, where money was tight, for instance, people would simply unbolt the stock VW wheels, remove the hubcap clips and bolt the rims back on, back to front. The effect of this was to widen the rear track - and make the car liable to lose a wheel as the lug nuts no longer seated correctly!

Whether or not to run with hubcaps was a matter of personal taste. More often than not, if hubcaps were fitted they were those "nipple" type from an early Porsche, complete with Stuttgart crest. In many instances, hubcaps would be fitted only on the front wheels, with the rear brake drums painted red or yellow to give a sporting look. At this time, almost every car ran with full bumpers and that meant complete with the US-specification "towel-rail" bumper bars.

As far as other external modifications went, there were few. The cars all retained their chrome trim, almost invariably sported a factory paintjob and relied on the stock lights and turn signals to stay legal. Jim Holmes's original ragtop Beetle was unusual in having a racing stripe down each side, but

**Ron Fleming's 1956 sedan was typical of the early cars with its Goodyear tires, American Racing mag wheels and single-color paintwork. Note how the car has retained all the original trim, including the bumpers and bumper guards.**
(Ron Fleming)

other cars in the club would sport signwritten logos for their favorite speedshop on the rear fenders. Most popular among these was an advertisement for Anchor Mufflers, the company responsible for bending up the equal-length exhaust headers often found on these early cars.

A few cars would be fitted with smoked Plexiglass (Lexan) inserts in the rear side windows for a touch of class with, maybe, a decal or two to hint at what was under the deck lid, or to show the owner's club affiliations. These inserts were often nothing more than pieces of Plexiglass cut to the shape of the window and secured against the inside by a few little pins pushed into the sealing rubber.

As for the ride height, that would stay exactly as the factory intended, or possibly a little higher, to

Dave Dolan's engine was typical of those fitted to the original California Look cars. A lightly-modified 1200, the motor has been fitted with a Bosch 010 distributor, Blue coil and a chrome velocity stack. Note Lions Dragstrip pit permit!
(Greg Bunch)

Don Crane bought his '67 brand new and immediately modified it with BRM wheels, Anchor Headers exhaust and a hot motor. Crane's sedan was the first street car to use 48IDA Weber carburetors and had blue-tinted side windows.
(Greg Bunch)

Jim Holmes ran this sedan in the mid-'60s. Porsche hubcaps with wheel trims on stock front wheels, chromed Porsche rims with red brake drums at the rear. Megaphone tip to glass-pack muffler was a common finishing touch.
(Greg Bunch)

By 1969, Ron Fleming's oval window Bug had changed dramatically with the addition of BRM wheels - here shown fitted with radial tires on the front and Hurst slicks on the rear. Slicks were for racing only, but no one seemed to care!
(Ron Fleming)

The bumpers had by now been permanently removed, but the car still kept all its trim and the exhaust cut outs in the rear valance have not yet been filled. "Bug/O" signwriting on decklid refers to "Bug Optional" drag class at Lions.
(Ron Fleming)

mimic the appearance of the drag race cars of the era. The idea of lowering your Volkswagen had not yet caught on.

Inside the car, modifications were, again, relatively few and simple. Dave Dolan's 1967 was typical in having a chromed ashtray, a set of wooden dashboard knobs (almost certainly EMPI) and little else. Some cars would sport wood-rimmed steering wheels, but most retained the original factory item. Usually, gear shifters were stock, fitted with either an EMPI-Speedwell Quickshift, or perhaps nothing more than an aftermarket wooden knob. Other interior trim tended to be factory in origin, although some did sport front seats from early Porsches which offered greater comfort and style. Rarely did funds stretch to having a full interior retrim. Instrumentation would be stock with just a tachometer added, only a few people opting to purchase a set of EMPI instruments at this time.

There were relatively few aftermarket parts available for VWs, and these didn't always find favor with the instigators of the California Look. EMPI is a name that has grown to be synonymous with the west coast VW scene of old, but in truth EMPI's products were often considered too dressy for most tastes. Aside from the Okrasa and other performance parts on offer, at this time the majority of EMPI's product range consisted of dress-up parts that were to form only a small part of the vestigial California Look. Only in later years did these early EMPI products become highly prized by collectors.

Mechanically, the original cars were fairly modest in specification, with a typical engine being a little 1200cc unit with bored out carburetor venturi, Bosch 010 distributor from an old VW bus (chosen because of its superior advance curve and all-centrifugal operation), slightly raised compression and possibly some reworked cylinder heads. A trip to

Pat at Anchor Mufflers would see a set of equal-length headers made to fit under the rear valance, while the muffler would be a glass-pack. These mufflers almost became an artform all of their own, with each member seemingly favoring a different tailpipe treatment. Dave Dolan tried dual mufflers at first, but liked neither the looks nor the resultant horsepower, so he came up with a glasspack set-up that exited to the right and sported a simple chromed megaphone tip. Don Crane's '67, however, had a system that exited to the left and featured a parallel-sided chrome muffler and tailpipe. Other variations included a simple large-diameter curved pipe that slipped over the top of a regular glasspack

**The Spyder - later referred to simply as the 8-spoke - became one of the most popular wheels of all time, fitting everything from Fastbacks and Squarebacks to late-model sedans like Dan Czapla's stunning burgundy Bug, shot in 1972.** (Ron Fleming)

and gave the impression that no muffler was fitted.

In these early days, speed equipment was not as readily available as it would be in years to come. As a result, most engine modifications relied on the owner's ingenuity or the advice offered by fellow club members. As is usual with most car clubs, a certain pooling of resources took place among members of DKP with, for example, Greg Aronson and Ron Fleming becoming the transmission experts. However, engine components were often purchased from Gene Berg in Orange (once he had made the move down from Washington) or Dean Lowry in Santa Ana. Engine Dynamics or Rimco were the chosen companies to carry out engine balancing or other machining services. For dress-up goodies and general parts, Auto Haus (founded by Ron Rosevaar) in Buena Park was popular, especially as John Lazenby, one of the original DKP club members, was general manager for over nine years.

The V8 enthusiast had been able to buy an impressive range of speed equipment since the 1940s, but it was to be some while before parts such as stroker crankshafts would become easily accessible

**When Volkswagen launched the 4-lug Beetle for the European market in 1967, the end of the road was in sight for the BRM wheel. EMPI came to the rescue with the GT Spyder which, like the earlier 5-spoke, had a two-piece rim.** (Author)

**Rick Winter's sedan was simple, yet attractive. Chromed Porsche wheels hark back to the formative days of the California Look, while dechromed bodywork brought it bang up to date in 1972 when this photograph was taken.**
(Ron Fleming)

**John Lazenby, a founder member of Der Kleiner Panzers, opted to use a set of rare American Racing 5-lug wheels on his *Butternut* sedan. Car featured body and paint by Becker and an interior by Don Bradford. Note brown ragtop.**
(Ron Fleming)

to VW owners. In the latter part of the 1960s, Greg Aronson and Ron Fleming recall making pilgrimages to Earl McMills in Inglewood, CA. McMills was the guy to go to to buy welded stroker crankshafts and reworked cylinder heads at a time when such parts were a pipedream for most people.

Carburetors such as the Zenith 32NDIX were original fitment on a variety of imported vehicles, including British Daimlers and French Simcas. Tom Lieb of Scat tried fitting one of these dual-throat carbs onto a modified VW manifold and came up with some extra horsepower as a result. It wasn't long before a single Zenith on a home-brewed manifold became a relatively common sight on hot VWs of the era as more and more people searched for the Holy Grail of horsepower.

Drag racers had long appreciated that, to get the maximum power out of an engine, an individual inlet port per cylinder was the way to go. When the Volkswagen factory introduced the dual-port cylinder heads on the Type 3 range in the mid-'60s, it was like a gift from God as far as VW hot rodders were concerned. Suddenly here was a mass-produced cylinder head that offered everything the older, more exotic, Okrasa head could but at a price that just about anyone could afford. After all, it didn't take long for these new heads to start showing up in wrecking yards! With dual-port heads, a whole new era of VW horsepower would begin, of which more anon. . . .

As time passed, so the accepted style of southern California VWs began to change, and one of the first areas under scutiny was the wheels. When EMPI announced its famous BRM wheel in June 1966, it was considered too expensive by many at just under $50 a piece. After a while, though, the wheel gained respect among the more serious pioneers of the California Look thanks to its light weight (a claimed saving of 3lbs 12oz per wheel) and increased rim width – to 5 inches – that would allow a fatter section tire to be mounted safely. Very soon it became *the* wheel to have and has remained so until this day.

Developed as a joint venture between Joe Vittone's EMPI and former world champion Graham Hill's Speedwell operation in England, the BRM wheel was cast out of 90% pure magnesium which made it at once both light and somewhat fragile. It was also very prone to corrosion. The story goes that if you polished your BRMs on Friday afternoon, by the time you went cruising that night they would look so bad you wouldn't want to show your face. With owners having to spend up to an hour – or more – polishing each wheel, a certain amount of dedication was called for! Bill "Wee Willie" Aroyo was the first in DKP to polish his BRMs to a mirror finish, using Brasso and wire wool to achieve the desired effect. Once one person showed up with mirror-finish BRMs, the rest soon followed suit.

However, not everyone fell for the unique looks of the BRM: Greg Aronson at first shunned the wheel, considering it ugly, only to change his mind at a later date. He was not alone in his thinking, but there was one thing which everyone agreed on and that was adaptors of any kind were out! If the wheel

couldn't be fitted to a Volkswagen brake drum without resorting to an adaptor of some kind then there was no place for it on your car.

The 5-lug BRMs had only a short production life as the Volkswagen factory introduced the 4-lug Bug for the US market in the 1968 model year (in Europe, the first 4-lug Bug had already been introduced in the form of the 1967 disc-braked 1500 model), so demand fell sharply. EMPI kept up with the changing times by introducing the 8-spoke GT Spyder wheel, which was a two-piece cast aluminum wheel designed to fit the new range of VWs. It was essentially an updated version of the earlier EMPI 5-spoke wheel which fitted the older 5-lug cars, but was available in both 14 and 15 inch diameters and with rims designed to accept either tubed or tubeless tires.

Although in more recent years the EMPI 5-spoke wheel has become an accepted part of the California Look, at first surprisingly few cars used them. Other wheels that were accepted and proved to be popular included the ET Mag, as used on Ron Fleming's '56, and the Rader – a steel-rimmed, cast aluminum-centred 5-lug wheel marketed by EMPI which gained recognition while used on the original *Inch Pincher* drag car.

Later still, as BRMs became scarce, people looked for alternatives. In that first California Look issue of *Hot VWs*, Dean Kirsten's '67 could be seen sporting a set of very light – and now equally rare – polished Deano aluminum racing wheels from DDS. Other choices came to include Porsche 911 forged alloy

**Porsche 914 wheels suddenly became popular in the latter part of the 1970s. Lowering the rear suspension was becoming more popular, too. Note Der Selten Käfers VW Association decal in side window of Matt Jahr's '64 sedan.** (Hot VWs)

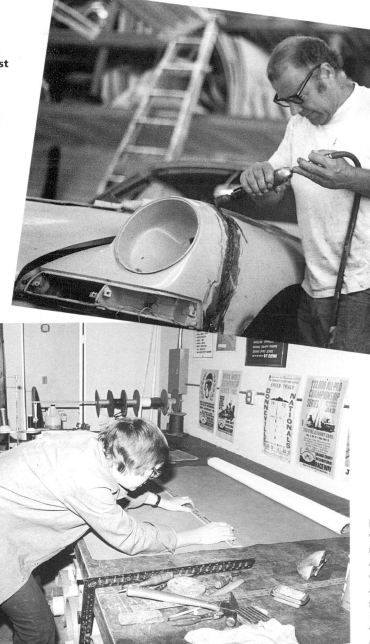

Leonard Becker ran Becker's Bug House in Orange and was always considered to be the first choice for quality paint and bodywork. Becker was the person responsible for welding up all 49 trim holes in Greg Aronson's white '63. (Ron Fleming)

Don "Brad" Bradford was, like Becker, the number one choice among members of the California Look scene. His attention to detail was second to none. Here he is cutting the material for the seats in Keith Goss's show-winning '62. (Dean Kirsten)

rims, Rivieras – as frequently seen on Porsche 914s – or wheels from Walker Wheels and Big Wheels. Very occasionally some early cars would be fitted with a pair of Ansen slot mags, often just on the rear – Aronson's car was so equipped in the early days – but they were not a common choice.

A gradual but constant evolution of these early California Look VWs could be seen throughout the late 1960s. At first there was the stock ride-height, bumpers, chrome trim, factory paintjob, mild single-carb engine and chrome wheels. By about 1969 this simple look had gradually transformed into something a little more akin to what is today accepted as the traditional California Look: bumpers began to disappear in an effort to save weight at the

Wednesday night grudge races at Orange County Raceway, engines became more highly tuned and mag wheels – especially BRMs – became more popular. Greater emphasis was placed on paintwork and interiors, and two names became pre-eminent: Leonard Becker and Don Bradford.

Becker was the proprietor of a paint and bodyshop on Lincoln in Orange whose Bug Shop specialized in repainting Volkswagens. His painting skills, and those of his employees, were second to none. In time, Leonard Becker would be the first to weld up all the trim holes in a VW to help create the classic dechromed California Look. In short, if you wanted a show-winning paintjob with bodywork to match, Becker's was the place to go. His

Bob Carmona's 1957 oval window sedan had an interior by Bob's Auto Trim. Plaid inserts became popular in the mid-'70s. VDO gauges and late-model 100mph speedometer help keep tabs on the 1700cc engine with dual 42DCNF Webers. (Jere Alhadeff)

Interior of Dean Kirsten's '67 sedan showing typical "Brad" upholstery with characteristic "fat biscuit" inserts in the seats and door panels. Motolita steering wheel, Deano Dyno-Soars gear shifter and racing harnesses finish it off. (Jere Alhadeff)

workmanship didn't come cheap, though, and Dean Kirsten recalls working at a print shop all summer long to save the $500 necessary to have his car prepped and painted at the Bug Shop. Becker's, of course, wasn't the only specialist VW paintshop in Orange County, for a number of high quality cars were to come out of Fivepoints in Huntington Beach.

Although the early cars may have largely retained the factory paintwork, by 1969 or '70 things started to change. Members of clubs like DKP began to experiment, not with the outrageous Metalflakes and Candys favored by others, but with simple, high quality single-colour paintjobs - especially bright reds, black, pure white or chrome yellows. Porsche India Red would remain one of the most popular choices for a long time for a California Look VW, especially a Bug.

In the same way that Leonard Becker's Bug Shop was not the only paintshop, Don "Brad" Bradford, whose trim shop was in Anaheim, may not have been the only upholsterer but he, too, earned himself an unparalleled reputation in VW circles. Brad's trademark came to be what were termed as "fat biscuits" - perfectly sewn rectangular designs in the seat and backrest inserts and door panels. Nobody could match the perfection of his double rows of parallel stitching or the fit of his headliners. Even when, in later years, a car was brought to him that had been roof-chopped, it would be impossible to distinguish between the fit of his custom headliner and that of a factory original. Other trademarks of Brad's included map pockets sewn into the fenderwell carpets - a practical feature on a Bug that may have lost its glove box due to a custom dashboard installation.

Everything about the handiwork of both Don Bradford and Leonard Becker was perfect and a

"Frenchy" De Houx's '67 Karmann Ghia had an eye-catching plaid Herculon interior by Jere Smith of Vee Dub Seat Covers. Inserts were surrounded by brown leather. Formuling France steering wheel was a popular choice. (Jere Alhadeff)

Keith Goss's chop-top sedan featured a pair of early Porsche 911 seats, trimmed in typical Don Bradford style. Goss's car differed from most by having a filled dashboard into which a full complement of VDO gauges has been set. Very classy. (Jere Alhadeff)

large number of top show cars over the years featured examples of their skills. It would not be unjust to say that, even to this day, their work has not been bettered. Sadly, neither business exists today and, particularly in the case of Brad, few complete examples of their handiwork survive untouched.

A whole new look to the interior of the cars began to develop. Several Bugs began to show with dashboards equipped with either VDO or Stewart-Warner gauges, the former being the more popular as they tended to give a Porsche-like feel to the car. Although these gauges were generally fitted into the speaker grill adjacent to the speedometer on an otherwise stock dashboard, some people began to follow the lead taken by Greg Aronson and cut out the original dash panel, replacing it with - in Aronson's case - Plexiglass, or aluminum sheet. Again, this added to the race-car look as well as allowing the owner freedom to place his extra gauges where he could most easily read them.

Small, leather-bound steering wheels became popular, too. Motolita or Britannia were the favored makes, although Formuling France would ultimately become the first choice. Gear shifts were either stock with an EMPI E-Z-R conversion or aftermarket parts from DDS or Hurst. DDS shifters were certainly considered to be the very best at the time.

Seats still tended to remain stock, albeit retrimmed, although some cars were fitted with aftermarket 'glass buckets trimmed in naugahyde for more of a race-car look. Others favored early Porsche 911 seats, but they never proved to be as popular as the original VW parts.

By around 1970, the traditional and now well-recognized California Look style had reached maturity, and one of the principal elements of the Look was the lowered front suspension. In these formative days only the front ride height was

Riviera wheels appeared on the scene in the late '70s and soon proved to be a favorite. Racing mirror was a commonplace accessory, but the treatment of the rear licence plate on Martin Durham's "MY72 VW" was unusual.
(Jere Alhadeff)

Ernie Barron's Porsche Sepia Brown 1968 sedan, unusually, retained its heavy Eurostyle bumpers. Porsche 911 Fuchs rims look right at home on a VW, but require the brake drums to be redrilled due to the different bolt pattern.
(Jere Alhadeff)

changed – the rear suspension remained at the factory settings. To lower the front end there was a variety of ways available, although removing some of the torsion bar leaves in the front beam was the favored method. To do this, the stub axles, king- and link-pin assemblies and trailing arms had to be removed. The torsion bars themselves could then be slid out of the axle beam and welded together in the centre and at each end. A hacksaw or grinder was used to cut out some of the leaves so as to soften the spring rate. The result was a hit-or-miss reduction in ride height, depending on how weak the torsion leaves had become over the years.

A slightly more sophisticated alternative was the Scat Select-A-Drop, which was a weld-on lowering device that allowed the lower torsion leaves to be twisted round in relation to the top set. At least with the Select-A-Drop it was possible to adjust the ride height with a pair of wrenches, but the ride quality suffered badly as a result of the stiffening of the torsion bars. In later years, the Sway-A-Way torsion bar adjuster became the industry standard, as it allowed the suspension to be lowered without undue loss of ride quality.

As far as shock absorbers are concerned, whenever the suspension is lowered it is necessary to fit a shorter than stock damper. At first there were no commercially available short shocks for the VW so owners of the post-'64 ball-joint Bugs were forced to modify Opel shock absorbers to fit their lowered cars. Koni shock absorbers were always the favored choice among the pioneers of the California Look thanks to their adjustability and excellent handling characteristics.

The biggest drawback with running a lowered Volkswagen was not, however, the matter of the loss of ride quality. When in stock form, the headlights of a VW Bug were right on the lower limits of the 24 inch minimum height law in California. Technically speaking, as soon as any VW was lowered by even one inch, then the law was broken and the owner would find himself liable to a traffic ticket. The harassment of California Look VWs became a popular sport among members of the

**"Try My '69"**, reads the slogan, but the propped open decklid, dual-muffler exhaust system and the sound of a pair of 48IDA Webers on a hot 1776cc motor would probably make most 'opponents' wary of tackling Geno Combs' Bug. (Jere Alhadeff)

**For some reason, EMPI's 5-spoke wheels took a while to become accepted, possibly because they were always somewhat overshadowed by the BRM. Note the Plexiglass covers over the headlights and early-style turn signals.** (Hot VWs)

Orange County police, with at least one member of Der Renwagen Fuhrers VW Club spending the night in jail for having the front end too low on his Bug!

Once a "fixer" ticket had been issued by a police officer it was necessary to visit your local station to have the ticket signed off and the car declared legal once again. Naturally, this would entail having to return the car to stock ride height - at least for the duration of the inspection. The usual trick would be to drive to a friend's house close to the Police Department, remove the front shocks and fit in their place a pair of rigid struts that would lift the front end up to the legal ride height. Then, once the car had been inspected and the ticket signed off, the struts would be removed and the shocks refitted back at the friend's house. As they say, where there's a will, there's a way. . . .

When Greg Aronson decided to dechrome his car, it was to smooth the lines of the bodywork and give the sedan the feel of a race car. Drag racers had already decided that chrome trim was superfluous, not only adding weight but also spoiling the airflow over the car. Once Aronson showed up with his chrome trim removed and the remaining holes welded up, the trend spread rapidly. Leonard Becker's original price tag of "a buck a hole" proved to be somewhat optimistic as his attempts to prevent heat distortion of the surrounding panels turned it into a very time consuming job. Later quotes were in the region of a more realistic $200-300!

Another race car feature that many tried to copy was the one-piece side window, doing away with the wind-wings for a smoother look. Several people attempted to make this work on a street car, retaining the roll-up windows by using home-spun ingenuity. Leonard Becker even gave up trying after a while, having explored the possibility of using

Jeff Lopez went against the flow when he built his 1961 California Look cabriolet. Convertible Bugs were never a popular choice, largely because no one ever really raced a cabriolet. However, no one can deny Jeff's car looked good. (Jere Alhadeff)

A popular color, Porsche India Red, and an uncommon choice of wheels: Big Wheels. These two-piece rims were made specifically for the 5-lug VWs but were never a popular choice. Note the buggy-bar on the front of Randy Welch's car. (Roger Grago)

winder mechanisms from an old split-window Bug. Some street cars adopted the one-piece window look by simply replacing the stock glass with a single sheet of Lexan, but that was a short-cut which didn't suit most people.

Eventually, in 1974, Dean Kirsten got to hear of a company, Frank's Glass in Bellflower, which had succeeded in coming up with a working solution to the problem. About one week before Bug-In 12, Kirsten took his blue '67 sedan up to Bellflower and had the conversion carried out. As a consequence, his was the first car seen at a Bug-In event with wind-up one-piece windows.

Along with falling foul of the law by lowering the front suspension, one other aspect of the California Look was guaranteed to bring about regular brushes with the local police: running without bumpers. In order to save weight at the drags, it was common for the owners of street-driven race cars to remove bumpers to save weight, unbolting them when they got to the track. Leaving

the bumpers off your VW became regular practice and rapidly spread throughout California Look circles.

When a law was introduced stating that every car had to be fitted with bumpers, people searched for ways to get round it. Close scrutiny of the wording showed all that was necessary was to have some form of protective structure that would prevent direct contact between the bodywork and another car. In theory, nothing more than a Coke bottle cap strapped to the rear decklid handle would have been legal, such was the absurdity of the law, a point raised by a colleague (who happened to be a police officer) of DRF member Dave Rhoads.

Ultimately, the problem of how to run legally without bumpers and yet still retain the slick good looks of the traditional California Look was solved by Greg Aronson. He made a set of aluminum nerf bars that bolted straight up to the stock bumper mounts; they satisfied the law and yet still looked good. This, however, was too late to save Dean

Kirsten from his brush with the law.

While attending Fullerton Junior College, he used to drive back and forth on Harbor Boulevard where the police would sit in waiting. He was regularly stopped and warned about the front end of his Bug being too low, but eventually got a ticket for running without bumpers. Until that point, Kirsten had never had a "fixer" ticket so was unaware of the procedures. The cop told him that he had to put the bumpers back on the car and report for an inspection at Fullerton Police Department, which he duly did. "Is that all I have to do?", asked Kirsten. "Yes - you're done", came the reply.

Six months later, there was a knock at the door of his parents' house at 7.00am one Sunday morning. On the doorstep was a police officer with an arrest warrant. Kirsten was handcuffed and thrown in the back of a police car unaware that, even though the ticket had been signed off, he was still required to attend court or at least call to see if there was a fine of some sort. He spent a night in jail, raised the $85 bail and paid an attorney a further $100, making this one of his more expensive introductions to California traffic law.

Aside from the purely aesthetic alterations, one area that really set true California Look cars aside from all others was what lay under the deck lid. As the Look had largely grown out of the world of drag

**Harvey Rosenthal's '66 displays the classic California Look rake - nose down, tail high. FAT Performance T-bars look right at home on this dechromed sedan. Wheels are American Racing fitted with a set of radial tires.**
(Roger Grago)

racing, it was inevitable that owners should have a fascination with horsepower. By the late '60s, long-stroke crankshafts and EMPI 88mm big-bore piston and cylinder kits had become popular with the racers while, on the street, the majority of owners favored fitting a set of "88s" with a stock VW crank for a nominal 1700cc engine.

If there had been a standard California Look engine, it would have been something like this: EMPI 88mm cylinders and pistons, dual-port cylinder heads fitted with 40mm x 35.5mm valves, a full porting job by FAT Performance or Fumio Fukaya, Engle 110 camshaft, a Bosch 010 distributor and a pair of 48IDA Weber carburetors on tall manifolds, operated by an EMPI or Berg linkage. Exhaust systems were usually tubular merged headers with, at first, a single "quiet" muffler, to be overtaken later by dual "quiets" as pioneered by FAT Performance in 1976. Engines such as these were commonplace in Orange County in the early 1970s and provided plenty of reliable fun for their owners.

Although by and large the simple 1700cc motor

Every fast street car worth its salt ran a pair of 48IDA Weber carburetors, more often than not mounted on tall Skat Trak manifolds. These carburetors were developed by Weber primarily for racing, and offered for use on VWs by EMPI. (Author)

Action from *Hot VWs* magazine's Drag Day 2 held in July 1978 at Orange County Raceway. A pair of classic California Look sedans streak across the finish line. Note the spun aluminum wheels, a popular choice by this time. (Hot VWs)

remained the most popular choice, there were several people who felt that there was no substitute for cubic inches and built far larger engines for their street cars. In 1970 Mike Mahaffey ran a 2180cc dual-Webered motor in his 1951 split-window Beetle, enabling it to run 12-second quarter miles in street trim. By anybody's reckoning that is extremely fast for a street car. However, it was Don Crane who

is credited as being the first person to fit a pair of 48IDA Webers to what was at the time a street car. Ron Fleming recalls the look of amazement on everyone's faces when Crane pulled these carbs out from under his bed - to anyone used to considering a pair of Solex 40P11s as being the ultimate, the sight of dual IDAs was one to savor!

As far as transmissions were concerned, certainly in the early days of the Look, the majority of cars ran with stock gearboxes. That was fine until it came time to exercise some horsepower, at which point the fragile stock differential would be one of the first parts to break, followed soon after by the axles. It wasn't long before people realized that, to get the

**Mike Mabe's awesome Karmann Ghia featured a 1600cc engine equipped with a Rajay turbo system developed by Dave Kawell of Kawell Racing Engines. Fittingly enough, the licence plate of this street legal Karmann read FAS GHIA.** (Rich Kimball)

most from their new found horsepower, it would be necessary to change the factory gear ratios for something a little closer.

Volkswagen had always intended that fourth gear should be something of an overdrive, designed to make for easy freeway cruising. However, the resultant gap between third and fourth gears, allied to the jump from second to third, meant that tuned VWs with high-lift, long-duration camshafts would go "off the boil" between shifts. By fitting close-ratio third and fourth gears, the gaps were closed up, allowing the engine to stay within the power band all the way up through the gears. The biggest drawback with this, however, was that cars so

**Kris Klingaman's '69 VW began life as an extremely fast street car, but gradually made the transition to all-out race car. Klingaman ran the blue sedan in NHRA B/MC competition and at the Bug-Ins and Drag Days at OCIR.** (Rich Kimball)

equipped became more tiring to drive over a long distance, as the low fourth gear tended to restrict freeway cruising speeds.

Whenever there is discussion of what constitutes a true California Look car, the subject of year of manufacture is not far behind. For many, the 1967 sedan is considered to be the ultimate but, if an eye is cast over California Look cars of the late '60s and early '70s, by far the most popular body style would

**As the California Look was inspired by what was happening on the drag strips, relatively few Karmann Ghias were given the treatment. "Frenchy" De Houx's stunning '67 helped to turn the tide of opinion in favor of the German coupés.**
(Jere Alhadeff)

be the '63 to '66 Bug. The reason the 1967 sedan has become so sought after is that at the time it was considered to be the last of the traditional Bugs, with its non-padded dashboard but with the benefit of 12v electrics (at least as far as the US market was concerned).

Don Crane bought a brand new '67 when they first became available, as did Dave Dolan's mother. Crane's car was ultimately to become a race car while Mrs Dolan's would end up in the hands of her son, who had persuaded her to part with her money for a VW in the first place. Dean Kirsten recalls the day his brother visited a VW dealership late in 1967 to purchase a new car but was persuaded by the salesman to wait a few months until the new models came in. He did and didn't like what he saw: the

**Three cars - six 48IDA Webers. The sedans of DKP's Stan Davis (left), Mark Thurber (center) and Rick Zavala all captured the very essence of the Look. Three different models of Bug united by a single desire: horsepower!**
(Ron Fleming)

padded dashboard, revised bodywork and ugly Euro bumpers all contrived to hide the simple lines that made the previous year's Bug so appealing.

To this day, the '67 Bug still has a strong following - former DKP President, Jim Edmiston, chooses to run a '67 some 20 years after he moved out of the club scene and took an interest in sand rails. With its Becker paintjob and neat interior, the car proves beyond doubt that while time may pass some things will never change.

Mike Mahaffey turned a deaf ear to the restorers when he decided to build his California Look sedan around a 1951 split-window Bug. BRM wheels and largely dechromed bodywork complement Concorde Green paintwork.
(Ron Fleming)

Mahaffey's '51 ran a 2180cc motor with dual 48IDAs to give it fearsome performance on the street. Although the bumpers have been removed, note that the cut-outs remain in the rear fenders. Photograph was taken in 1972 at a DKP gathering.
(Ron Fleming)

# CALIFORNIA LOOK CARS
## A CLOSER LOOK AT SOME OF THE MOST SIGNIFICANT CARS OF THE '70S

The California Look style may have evolved over a period of years, but it is still generally recognized that there was one vehicle above all others that stands as a statement of what the Look is all about: the 1963 sunroof sedan of Greg Aronson.

Aronson - "Youngie" to his friends - was a member of the original Der Kleiner Panzers VW Club and formed a partnership with Ron Fleming which eventually led to the setting up of FAT Performance. He first acquired the sedan from an old gentleman in Garden Grove. It was still painted the original colour, Basalt Grey, with a matching grey ragtop.

Soon after, Aronson painted the car metallic brown with a tan top. The interior was, in Aronson's own words, pretty ugly, the dashboard being redone in black wrinkle finish paint with a row of idiot lights along the top. Externally, the sedan wore a pair of Ansen Sprint slot mags on the rear, fitted using adaptors (normally a no-no in DKP!), while at the

**On a caravan to San Diego zoo in 1968, Greg Aronson's 1963 ragtop sedan (on left) cruises alongside Ron Fleming's '56. Already the beginnings of a new style can be seen, with Aronson favoring narrower tires and a lower ride height.**
(Ron Fleming)

front Porsche-style chrome rims were used. To give the car a little more power, Don Crane and Ron Fleming built Aronson a warmed-up 40hp motor with a 1350cc big-bore conversion which was used for a while, including trips to Lions drag strip.

At one of the DKP Drag Days down at Carlsbad Raceway, a fellow club member won a Scat Select-A-Drop lowering device. At that point, everyone in the club had their cars raised so it wasn't an especially sought after prize. Aronson carried out some work on his colleague's car and, in return, he was given the Select-A-Drop. He drove over to a dune buggy shop in Garden Grove where it was fitted to the '63 and the front end duly lowered.

The old and the new: Mark Thurber's brown sedan still wears its factory chrome trim and stock ride height, while Aronson's lacks its trim and, thanks to a Select-A-Drop, has its nose firmly down in the weeds. Photo taken around 1970. (Ron Fleming)

The car was fitted with a glassfiber decklid, an unusual feature for the time. Aronson had taken time to mold in the original hinge mechanism so the new lid opened and shut just like a stock decklid. The tires are Goodyear Blue Streaks. (Greg Aronson)

The classic California Look stance is shown to perfection in this photograph; stock rear ride height and radically lowered front end give the white sedan a purposeful, nose-down, hot rod rake, just like the drag race cars of the era. (Greg Aronson)

However, a second significant change to the car had yet to happen. Aronson took the car to Becker's Bug House in Orange where he asked Leonard Becker to weld up all 49 trim holes in the car. Becker had no idea what to charge, so suggested a price of one dollar per hole plus an extra buck, making $50 in all, but he soon realized that the deal was not a good one as far as he was concerned, the job proving to be a lot more time-consuming than he first imagined.

In 1969, with the bodywork now devoid of chrome, it was time for paint. Aronson chose what has been termed "appliance white" but was in fact 1968 Chevy truck white, which contrasted strongly with the new black sunroof and fender beadings. The decklid was replaced with a glassfiber one, complete with air scoop, and Aronson took great pains to ensure that it fitted well. He even molded in the original factory hinges from the old decklid so that it functioned correctly. To begin with, the car ran without bumpers of any sort, but eventually a set of FAT aluminum T-bars was added.

The interior was equipped with glassfiber seats which, although they looked racy, proved to be somewhat uncomfortable. Aronson also cut out the original dashboard and fitted a black Plexiglass insert in its place, although the glovebox was still retained complete with its own Plexiglass lid. A set of gauges

The interior of Aronson's car showing the black Plexiglass dashboard, VDO gauges and Grant sports steering wheel. The seats were glassfiber buckets trimmed in black vinyl, the passenger side one being hinged to allow access to the rear. (Jere Alhadeff)

To begin with, Aronson built a 1700cc engine with dual 48IDA Webers, Engle 110 camshaft and an SPG roller-bearing crankshaft. This was later replaced by an 1800cc engine with an Engle 130 camshaft and 10.5:1 compression. (Ron Fleming)

was fitted which comprised a VDO 8,000rpm tachometer, matching speedometer and oil pressure and temperature gauges. A Berg shifter, Grant steering wheel and a chromed ashtray completed the new look.

At first the revamped car ran a set of chrome rims, with Aronson borrowing Ron Fleming's BRM wheels when he showed it. He began the search for a set of BRMs, despite having initially considered them to be the ugliest wheels he had ever seen. When fellow club member Don Crane first acquired a set for his red '67 sedan, Aronson thought he was crazy, particularly as he had straight-swapped his chrome rims for the BRMs which an old lady had on her GTV Bug. She even paid to have a tire shop swap the wheels over! For tires, Aronson ran Pirelli Cinturatos, 135 section on the front with 165s on the back.

The quest for horsepower led Aronson to build a 1700cc motor with dual 48IDA Webers, an Engle 110 camshaft, Kolbenschmidt 88mm cylinders and an SPG roller crankshaft. With this combination, the

**A rare photograph of Jim Holmes, who purchased the car from Aronson, taking a trip down the OCIR quarter mile at a Bug-In. At this time, the sedan was fitted with a 1700cc Weber motor in characteristic California Look fashion.**
(Dean Kirsten)

car ran a 14.17-second quarter mile. He then stepped up to an 1800cc engine with an Engle 130 cam, 10.5:1 compression ratio, a close-ratio transmission and a pair of recapped slicks. A further trip to the drag strip resulted in a 13.50 timing slip. In Aronson's words, it was a real bear to drive on the street with such a high-lift, long-duration camshaft coupled with the close-ratio gears. He therefore replaced the camshaft with another Engle 110, lowered the compression ratio and then rebuilt the transmission with stock gear ratios.

With Pirellis back on it, the car still ran a healthy 13.86-second quarter mile. The milder engine and transmission combination had resulted in a car that was almost as fast but a lot easier to drive on the street. Soon after, however, Aronson felt the need to race the car a little more seriously again and rebuilt the engine with a 78mm Okrasa crankshaft, Porsche rods and an Engle 140 camshaft. The close-ratio

transmission went back in the car and, in this fourth incarnation, the sedan ran a 12.90. The fastest it ever ran, 12.73secs/105mph, was when Greg borrowed the transmission and slicks from Ron Fleming's *Underdog* race car.

Aronson feels that the prime reason for building the car the way he did was purely to be different rather than, as is commonly believed, to simply emulate what was happening on the drag strip. Certainly the timing of events bears this out: in 1969, when the car was lowered, the majority of drag race cars competed with unchanged ride height and suffered severe handling difficulties as a result. Aronson always felt that the car's strongest styling point was the contrast between the pure white of the paintwork and the black of the interior, ragtop and fender beading. Other club members reacted quite strongly to the car, the overall feeling being that this was something new and worth copying.

An out-take of the classic February 1975 *Hot VWs* cover. The denim-clad owner is Jim Holmes, his unimpressed "girlfriend" is Linda Dill, then Circulation Director of *Hot VWs*. Photo was taken close to the magazine's office in Costa Mesa.
(Jere Alhadeff)

Dave Rhoads' 1964 sedan is a real throwback to the days when horsepower was king. No chrome, polished aluminum T-bars, dual-muffler exhaust system and a Der Renwagen Fuhrers decal in the back window - all make a statement.
(Author)

One little known fact about this car is that it once beat the EMPI *Inch Pincher* of Darrell Vittone on the strip. With the white '63 in tow behind DKP member Craig Foster's Squareback panel van, Aronson made the trek up to Seattle, Washington, to compete in a drag race. He made his way through eliminations and found himself in the final against Vittone. As EMPI had part sponsored the event, the prize for winning the eliminations was a quantity of EMPI products. As his family owned EMPI, the prize held no interest for Vittone so he agreed to throw the race away and let Aronson's '63 take the win! How many other street cars can claim to have beaten the mighty *Inch Pincher*?

Eventually Aronson became tired of the VW scene and, like Fleming, bought a Porsche. The white '63 was purchased in late 1970 by fellow club member Jim Holmes, the wheels and engine being sold to other parties. Holmes searched out another set of BRMs to replace the chrome rims and had Fleming & Aronson build another 1700cc dual 48IDA motor.

The front suspension has been lowered and the car fitted with a prized set of BRM wheels. Green paint was first added in 1973, later redone about 10 years later. Rhoads' VW sees regular street use as well as drag strip action. (Author)

The 1994cc engine features an 82mm Tony Mance crankshaft, 88mm Mahle cylinders and pistons, 48IDA Webers and an Engle 130 camshaft. Cylinder heads have been reworked by Roger Crawford of Heads Up Performance. (Author)

Interior of Rhoads' '64 features padded dashboard with full set of VDO gauges. Gear shifter is a Gene Berg - the switch operates a line-lock, a device that allows the front brakes to be locked on while performing a burnout.

BRM wheels are used, spares being fitted with 26x6x15 Firestone slicks for drag race use. Just visible in this photograph is the traction bar fitted under the back of the engine to help prevent wheel hop at the drag strip. (Author)

Don Bradford working on the interior of Goss's car prior to Bug-In 16. Just visible behind Brad are the scratch-built mounts for the Porsche seats. Brad was without doubt the best of the automotive retrimmers in Orange County.
(Dean Kirsten)

It was in this form that the car came to be featured in the February 1975 issue of *Hot VWs* magazine - some four years or more since it had been built. In hindsight it seems strange that the car credited with having set the California Look rolling received no public recognition while it was owned by the person who was responsible for its construction. It never even appeared in any magazine photograph during Aronson's period of ownership. Sadly, today the car bears little resemblance to the way it looked in the early 1970s, having been stripped of its original interior and wheels.

Indeed, survivors of the halcyon days of the classic California Look are few and far between but some cars did manage to escape being rebuilt or crashed and stand today as reminders of what the VW scene in the early to mid-'70s was all about. Two such cars are the 1964 sedan of DRF member Dave Rhoads and the Bug-In winning 1962 chop-top sedan built by Keith Goss.

Rhoads' Bug was purchased early in 1970, following a visit by its owner to Bug-In 3 at Orange County Raceway where he witnessed the Schley brothers crashing their original *Lightning Bug*. The VW was the first automobile that the 18 year old Rhoads had ever owned and, before too long, it was destined to become a fast street car. To begin with the car was painted plain white. Rhoads lowered the front end and fitted a set of chrome rims with Porsche hubcaps, turning it into a perfect example of an early California Look car in the making.

However, it wasn't long before the stock engine was pulled from the car to make way for a 1700cc unit with dual 48IDA Weber carburettors, all hooked up to a stock transmission. In this form the sedan recorded a healthy 14.20sec/95mph at Orange County in the owner's hands.

Dave drove the car regularly, adding a set of original EMPI 5-spoke wheels which helped to complete the "Look". He also joined a Volkswagen club, choosing Der Renwagen Fuhrers over the rival Der Kleiner Panzers, and proceeded to attend just about every Volkswagen event on the calendar.

The car remained in pretty much the same configuration for several years, with the exception of being painted green in 1973. However, six years later, the Bug was stolen. It was found about a month later, stripped of its engine, transmission, interior and wheels. All the hard-to-get EMPI parts had been lost forever. Rhoads couldn't believe that this had happened to his car and, although it was not covered by theft insurance, he decided right away that the '64 would be rebuilt.

He began to build a 2-litre motor based around a Rimco-machined crankcase, 88mm Mahle cylinders and pistons, Tony Mance 82mm wedgemated crankshaft and a set of reworked stock VW conrods (these were later changed for some more durable Carillos). The 1994cc engine featured a pair of 48IDA Weber carburetors on tall Skat Trak manifolds and an Engle 130 camshaft. A pair of Volkswagen dual-port cylinder heads were fully reworked by Roger Crawford, a fellow DRF member and owner

**May 2nd 1976 - to the victor the spoils. Keith Goss (in yellow T-shirt) looks suitably pleased to have been presented with the Best Of Show trophy at Bug-In 16. On the right is Jeff Benedict whose own Karmann Ghia would win top honors a year later.**
(Keith Goss)

of Heads Up Performance in Fullerton. Crawford was also the owner and driver of the successful *Bad Company* drag race car. He welded and ported the heads and modified them to accept a set of 40mm x 35.5mm valves and stronger valve springs. With a compression ratio of 10.1:1 the engine produced some 180bhp at 7,000rpm on Crawford's dynamometer.

To cope with the power of the engine, the transmission was rebuilt with close-ratios and heavy-duty components throughout. In this form the car proved capable of running 12.40secs/105mph over the quarter mile, despite retaining the original steel body panels throughout. In fact, the only concession to weight loss was the replacement of the original bumpers with four lightweight aluminum T-bars, and a set of much-prized BRM wheels.

The interior of the car is very much a reflection of the era in which it was built, with a padded dashboard insert sporting a full complement of VDO gauges. The factory seats have been retrimmed in black velour and naugahyde, as have the door panels, while for greater driver safety the '64 now sports a roll bar and full TRW racing harnesses.

Dave Rhoads' car is one of the few to have survived the struggle against all odds, remaining to this day a perfect example of what a true California Look car should look like. It is a classic in every sense: dechromed bodywork, lowered stance, BRM wheels, hot motor, close-ratio transmission and finishing touches such as the T-bars and VDO-gauged dashboard, all serving to remind us of what it

was all about. Today the car still sees regular street and strip action, some 20 years after it first cruised the roads of Orange County.

Very few street-legal Volkswagens emulated their drag strip counterparts by succumbing to a roof chop - the process of removing a few inches from the overall roof height of the vehicle. On the drag strip, roof-chopped VWs became a familar sight once it had been proved beyond doubt that there were aerodynamic gains to be had by carrying out such surgery. *Inch Pincher II* was one of the first, followed by the Schleys' *Lightning Bug II* and Aronson's *Tar Babe* but, as far as road cars were concerned, it wasn't until Keith Goss came along that roof chops started to gain a wider appeal.

In 1975 Goss was working part-time at Fleming, Aronson & Thurber in Anaheim. He drove a tired 1962 VW sedan which was the butt of many jokes but it got him to and from work and that was all that mattered. However, being around the likes of Fleming and Aronson, the desire to build something special soon rubbed off on him. Images of *Tar Babe* flashed though his mind and he decided to build an all-out California Look Volkswagen with a difference: it would be roof-chopped.

Greg Aronson offered his support and gave Goss a brief lesson in welding before turning him loose on the car. He cut the roof off with a grinder and began measuring up how and where to cut. The problem with carrying out this modification to a Volkswagen Bug is that the roof needs to be stretched once the pillars have been shortened to

Keith Goss's car - now owned by the author - was one of the first roof-chopped sedans to hit the street. Influenced by drag race cars such as Greg Aronson's *Tar Babe*, the '62 was a show-stopper when it was first built back in 1976. (VolksWorld)

Once the car had been built and driven for a short while, Keith Goss removed the body and completely detailed the whole chassis to show standard. Every nut and bolt was replaced with a genuine VW part and cadmium plated for protection. (R K Smith)

Goss took home the trophies for Full Custom (left) and America's Most Beautiful Volkswagen. Awards were presented by Auto Haus and Don Burns Volkswagen respectively. Bug-In trophies were always bigger and better! (Author)

The finished interior is a work of art. Brad's trademark "Fat Biscuit" design can easily be seen here. The parallel rows of double stitching set his work apart from that of other less skilled upholsterers. Note the DDS shifter and Britannia wheel. (VolksWorld)

enable them to line up correctly. The normal practice is to use the roof off a second car to add the length, or to fabricate fill-in strips from sheet metal to close up the gaps. Goss tried the second method first, but was unhappy with the result, so removed the roof and repeated the procedure. He was still unsure when somebody suggested that he use the front half of the roof of a second car, so as to reduce the number of welds on the recontoured body.

The end result was perfect. It was one of the very few roof-chopped cars that retained the original lines of the Bug when viewed from the side. Even the decklid still lined up perfectly – the measure of a well thought out roof chop.

With the major bodywork carried out, Keith Goss took the car across to AJ's Bodyshop in Santa Ana where the front quarter panels were deseamed, the trim holes welded up and the decklid equipped with a pair of EMPI-like eyebrow vents in steel. The front and rear decklid handles were also removed, the engine cover being converted to cable operation. The dashboard was cut out of the

Engine is a 2160cc unit with an 84mm Okrasa crankshaft, Porsche 912 rods and 90.5mm Mahle pistons. Heads were reworked by Fumio Fukaya with 42mm x 37mm valves to suit 48IDA Weber carbs. Power output is in the region of 160bhp. (VolksWorld)

**Hot VWs Drag Day at Irwindale and Keith Goss heats up the tires on the chop-top sedan. Goss was never afraid to drive his car hard, even though it was good enough to win a show at any time. Best ET was a healthy 12.34 recorded at OCIR.**
(Dean Kirsten)

bodyshell and a flat piece of sheet metal welded in place. This was then cut to accept a full set of VDO gauges. From AJ's, the sedan was trailered over to Becker's Bug House where Leonard Becker applied several coats of Porsche Sahara Beige. Back at Goss's home, the body was reassembled with black fender beading and T-bars from FAT Performance.

The chassis was separated from the body and stripped to bare metal before being sprayed gloss black. The front axle beam was fitted with a Select-A-Drop and several of the suspension components, front and rear, chrome plated. The chassis was rebuilt using new parts throughout, including braided steel brake lines, Koni shock absorbers and a set of Porsche 356 drum brakes. Later the front drums would be replaced with a pair of Porsche 356C disc brakes. For rolling stock, the chop-top emerged from Goss's garage with a set of Porsche 911 Fuchs forged aluminum wheels shod with Pirelli radial tires, which necessitated having the brake drums redrilled to take into account the different bolt pattern of the wheels.

With the body reunited with the chassis, the '62 found its way into Brad's Upholstery shop where Don Bradford retrimmed a pair of early Porsche 911 reclining seats in beige naugahyde with his trademark "fat biscuit" inserts. The rear seat was cut down in height to make up for headroom lost with the roof chop and then, along with the door panels, trimmed to match the front seats. Carpets in brown, with Brad's fenderwell map pockets, a DDS shifter and a Britannia wheel completed the picture.

As far as the engine and transmission were concerned, the FAT Performance influence rubbed off once more. The 2160cc motor comprised an Okrasa 84mm crankshaft, 90.5mm Mahle cylinders, Porsche 912 conrods, 42mm x 37.5mm cylinder heads by Fumio Fukaya, Engle F48C camshaft, EMPI 1.4:1 rocker arms and dual 48IDA Webers. With its 9.0:1 compression ratio, the engine produced some 165bhp on FAT Performance's dynamometer. A close-ratio gearbox was built for the car, featuring a Crown differential and race axles. With this powerful yet strong combination, Goss's car covered the Orange County's quarter mile in 12.43 seconds. One interesting feature of the chop-top was that it was fitted with the first dual "quiet" muffler set-up seen on a VW. Fabricated by Ron Fleming, it showed the way ahead as far as exhaust system design was concerned.

The beautiful chop-top sedan was finally completed in the small hours of May 2nd 1976 with the help of Goss's friend Jeff Benedict, whose own Karmann Ghia was destined to take top Bug-In honours a year later. Later that morning the Bug was driven though the gates of Bug-In 16 and immediately drew the attention of a large crowd. At the awards ceremony the proud owner was handed a trophy inscribed "America's Most Beautiful Volkswagen" - his car had won Best Of Show.

Goss continued to drive the car up until 1984, when one of the Porsche conrods broke - a not uncommon failure. The engine was removed, rebuilt but never refitted. The Bug, whose California licence plate read *Chopped*, then lay under a dust sheet until November 1993 when it was purchased by the author. The Bug-In winning '62 chop-top now resides in England, looking exactly as it did the day it rolled through the gates of Bug-In 16.

# THE VW IN DRAG RACING

## THE AMAZING BUT TRUE STORY OF THE VOLKSWAGEN
## IN THE ROLE OF GIANT KILLER

There can be no accurate way of telling when the first Volkswagen ever made a trip down the drag strip, or who drove it. It may have been in southern California (as is most likely) but it could have just as easily happened on the east coast, where Volkswagens also had a strong following.

EMPI's *Inch Pincher* certainly campaigned in National Hot Rod Association (NHRA) competition as early as 1964, and prior to that Gene Berg and Dean Lowry had each been trying their luck with VW-powered machinery since the very early '60s. However, Volkswagen racing *per se* did not really get off the ground until the mid-1960s, when an increasing number of Bugs began showing up at the track, many of them owned by members of the original Der Kleiner Panzers VW Club. Some of the members would strip their cars out, removing the

back seat, bumpers and muffler (fitting a stinger tailpipe in its place) in an effort to save weight. They would then flat tow them across town to Lions and race against each other in the ET brackets – ie classes based on the elapsed times each car was capable of running. Others would drive their cars to the track and strip them of their excess weight in the pits. Up to 15 or 20 cars would often show up for these early competitions and the track even marked out a specific pit area for the VWs.

1967 was the turning point – both the NHRA

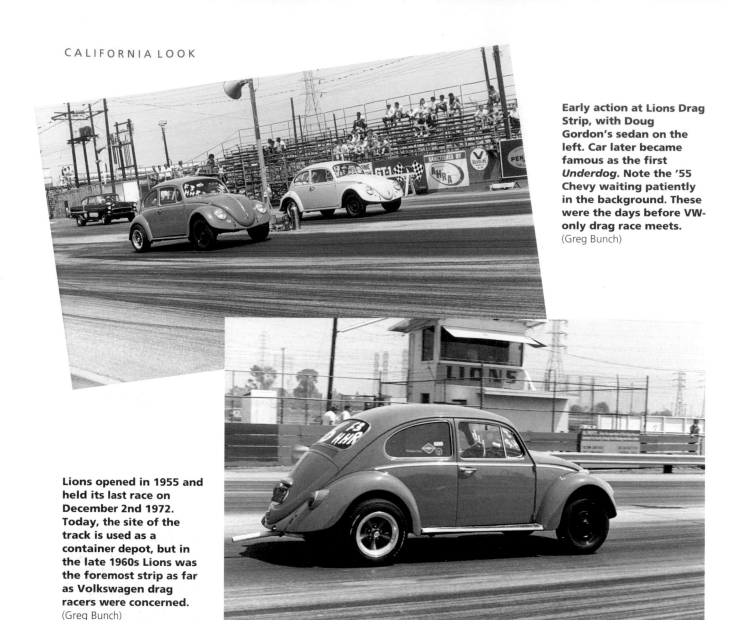

Early action at Lions Drag Strip, with Doug Gordon's sedan on the left. Car later became famous as the first *Underdog*. Note the '55 Chevy waiting patiently in the background. These were the days before VW-only drag race meets.
(Greg Bunch)

Lions opened in 1955 and held its last race on December 2nd 1972. Today, the site of the track is used as a container depot, but in the late 1960s Lions was the foremost strip as far as Volkswagen drag racers were concerned.
(Greg Bunch)

and Lions drag strip created three classes specifically for VWs. At Lions, these were Bug/Optional (36hp or 40hp, single- or two-barrel carburetor), 1300/1500 Sedan (Stock) and Unlimited. At the time, the majority of people would compete in the Bug/Optional class, which saw cars run high 18 or low 19 second times. The quickest Stock class competitor was Mike "Banana" Bonilla in his silver '68 sedan, which ran 17.70/17.80 thanks to some mild tuning: an S&S Dyno exhaust system and a power-pulley, along with the inevitable lightening (rear seat, bumpers, etc). In the Unlimited class, Don Crane's red '67 sedan ran high 15s and low 16s, having been rebuilt with a 78mm welded crankshaft and dual Solex 40P11 carburetors.

Vehicle preparation was kept to a minimum thanks to the very basic regulations, with no need for roll cages to be fitted unless the vehicle was capable of running quicker than 13-second quarter miles. Just about every car showed up with at least lap belts fitted, many having lap and diagonal seat belts – some DKP members even showed up with

full racing harnesses in their cars. The word "Stock" was loosely interpreted, with mild engine tuning being allowed along with the aforementioned lightening. Basically, everybody was just racing for fun and there were few complaints about infringements of the somewhat basic rule book.

In the same year that Lions initiated a VW-only racing class, so did the NHRA. Aware that there was an ever-increasing number of VWs showing up at other tracks, the NHRA was keen to take things under its wing. A new sub-committee was formed in its Charter Club Program to look after the Volkswagen drag racers, with EMPI's Dean Lowry as its principal adviser. The Riverside Volkswagen Association was formed by EMPI as the charter club, under the guidance of Rick Seol. On October 21st 1967, at the newly-opened Orange County Raceway (the track had only held its first meeting a few weeks earlier), the first ever NHRA-sanctioned race meeting for Volkswagens took place.

Three ET-based brackets were available: 13.75 to 18.50 seconds; 18.50 to 20.00 seconds and 20.00

Early Drag Day action at Carlsbad with "Dirty" Dave Vanderbeke leaving the line in the Renfree Motors-backed sedan. In the background is Dean Lowry's Ford Econoline tow vehicle and *Deano Dyno-Soar* race car. (Hot VWs)

seconds and up. "Each driver will be required to declare the elapsed time he wishes to be dialled into, prior to the eliminations. Racing will be round robin for the winner. A second round robin will be run, with the winner sitting out, for the runner-up. Each of the winners and runners-up will then run a third time for overall eliminator", stated the pre-event publicity. Class sponsors included Stewart Warner (overall eliminator), Cragar Industries (class winners), Champion (class winners), STP (winners and runners-up) and EMPI (winner of the 20.00 and up class). In addition, Orange County International Raceway donated trophies to each of the winners.

Over 60 Volkswagens showed up for NHRA's first ever VW-only drag race and racing didn't finish until after midnight! Gene Kibler, a familiar face at VW drag races in years to come, ended the day as "Mr Bug Eliminator", driving the Cotton Goff-sponsored '67 sedan to an 18.45sec/72.34mph final round win.

At this time Volkswagens were already running in the NHRA Gas classes, which were based on weight per cubic inch (lbs/ci) - "gas" being a reference to the fuel. The most popular of these were H/Gas and I/Gas, which were open to "pre-1960 flathead V8s, in-line and opposed 6-cylinder, straight-8s and in-line or opposed 4-cylinder engines with any type head". The weight breaks were 8.00-10.99 lbs/ci (H/Gas) and 11.00 or more lbs/ci (I/Gas). The only reason why VWs didn't enter in other gas classes where they would have been eligible, such as G/Gas

Pomona 1970, National Volkswagen Racing Association. Background (left to right): Doug Gordon, Bill Harmond, Rick Anderson, Dave Vanderbeke. Foreground: Dean Lowry, Bill Clarkson, Paul Schley, Ron Fleming, John Smith, Richard Bays, unknown, 'Mike', 'The Animal', Roy Jimenez. (NHRA)

(6.00 lbs/ci), is that the engines were too small in capacity to allow the cars to be competitive. The alternative would have been to reduce the weight to 800lbs, a physical impossibility if a Volkswagen was to remain legal in all other respects.

H/Gas racers of the early 1970s included the Schley brothers' *Lightning Bug*, Lowry's *Deano Dyno-Soar*, Skipp Hamm's *NED-Bug* and Bill Clarkson's

In March 1970, Dean Lowry found out the hard way about the aerodynamics of a VW Bug. At Sears Point Raceway in northern California, *Deano Dyno-Soar* was caught by a crosswind at the top end of the track, with disastrous results.
(Dean Lowry)

Audley Campbell owned Stuttgart High Performance Center and raced this chop-top K/Gasser to promote his business. Driven initially by Campbell, the *Stutt Bee* was later driven - as seen here at the 1974 Winternationals - by Paul Schley. (NHRA)

When roof-chops were in! 1972 Summernationals at Englishtown, New Jersey. Jack Kessel (foregeound), Jim Carlson (who took over from Darrell Vittone after the sale of EMPI), Denny Grove (NED Bug) and the Schleys line up. (NHRA)

*Iguana.* The front-running cars ran well down into the 'elevens', the quickest being Dean Lowry's with an 11.54. Amongst the heavier I/Gas cars was Darrell Vittone in *Inch Pincher II*, which held the class record of 12.12. Fastest of all the VW racers at the time was Richard Bays in his *Little Giant Killer* Porsche-powered Fiat 600 which sped through the traps at an amazing 112mph. Weight-wise, most H/Gas cars tipped the scales at around 1100lbs, while I/Gassers weighed in at around 1370lbs.

In addition to the above, the NHRA also instigated an 'MV' (Modified Volkswagen) class which allowed an "extensively modified body and chassis". The only provisos were that the vehicle had to be powered by a VW engine, with a single 2-barrel or dual single-barrel carburetors, and meet all the safety regulations that applied to the Gas classes. A/MV ran with a weight break of 15.00–19.99 lbs/ci, while B/MV allowed 20.00 or more lbs/ci. A typical

A/MV Bug might have been an 1835cc car weighing around 1700lbs, while for B/MV those figures would read 1500cc and 1820lbs respectively.

Later, in 1973, the class designation changed to A/MC and B/MC - short for "Modified Compact" - and thrown open to all four-cylinder compact cars with original equipment engines of 140ci (2294cc) or less, with a maximum of 151.5ci (2482cc) allowed for overboring. This soon became the happy hunting ground of many front-running VWs, including the Berg family's famous black '67 sedan and Tayco's very successful *Madness*. The Modified Compact classes lasted until 1984, when they were finally dropped by the NHRA.

Volkswagens became the scourge of the Gas classes, so much so that there was a lot of controversy about why the rules appeared to be written in favor of the little German sedans. In 1975 the rule book was extensively rewritten in favor of

**The *NED-Bug* was campaigned by Denny Grove from Pennsylvania. Car was destroyed in August 1971 in a massive accident at Niagara Drag Strip, NY after just six short months of competition. Grove escaped unhurt.** (Hot VWs)

the heavier domestic vehicles, and in 1978 the new V6 engines from General Motors were allowed in.

There had been much correspondence in the NHRA's own newspaper, *National Dragster*, on the subject of rules. One bone of contention was that with the way the Gas class regulations were written (". . .opposed 4-cylinder engines with any type of head"), Volkswagens could run legally with dual-port Okrasa-type cylinder heads, whereas other makes had to rely on stock castings.

Owners of old Chevrolet 6-cylinder and Ford flathead powered cars were outraged by this and bombarded *National Dragster* with letters to that effect. Matters were made worse for a while when the NHRA allowed a new design of Chevy straight-6 into the class (an engine that had previously been outlawed under the "pre-1960" ruling). With almost immediate effect, every old Chevy and all the Ford flatheads were rendered uncompetitive. Bowing to pressure, the "new" engine was outlawed again,

bringing about uproar from those Chevy lovers who had sold their old engines to buy a new model and then found themselves ineligible to race.

One letter summed it all up: *"I have just read this week's* National Dragster *and the results of the Winternationals drag races and I was appalled at the speeds of the winner of H/Gas class. I thought that NHRA changed the H/Gas class rules to only allow pre-1960 'sixes' to run this class because the late overhead 'sixes' had too much advantage over the older 'sixes'? So what happens is the late 'sixes' were banned from H/Gas to allow an even faster car to dominate the class and make it even worse than before.*

*"The VWs with the Porsche-type cylinder heads are now allowed to run this class unchallenged because there isn't a 'six' made today that can out-perform the VW-Porsche type car as indicated at this last Winternationals meet. The EMPI-powered VW car turned a fantastic ET of 12.76 during practice runs and won his class with a 12.92secs/95.64mph run. The losing VW only turned 13.01secs/99.66mph, which shows you that the winner was shutting off after beating his competition. . .*

*"To make this class a fair class for all cars, let us ban the use of the Porsche-type design heads and make all cars in this class run STOCK PRODUCTION heads with the stock number of ports."*

Ever the innovator, Dave Kawell was determined to disprove all the old wives' tales about how Karmann Ghias were unsuited to drag racing. Regular 11-second timing slips showed the sceptics that he was right and they were wrong. (NHRA)

Drag racing has always been hard on parts, and never more so than in the early days of VW drag racing. The use of high compression ratios and modified factory conrods frequently resulted in catastrophic engine failures such as this! (Hot VWs)

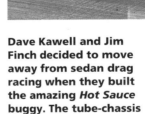

Even *National Dragster* couldn't come up with a good answer to that letter, suggesting that everyone with a grievance wrote to their NHRA divisional directors to bring about a rule change.

Eventually, the NHRA bowed to pressure brought to bear by the major domestic manufacturers. With new weight breaks and minimum weight limits, the VW was driven from the NHRA championships. By 1981 the party was well and truly over for the VWs when the NHRA introduced a 2100lbs minimum weight in I/Gas. Sadly, a lot of this was to do with the fact that Volkswagen, unlike any other motor manufacturer whose products triumphed at drag racing, showed no interest in what was going on. The company steadfastly refused to become financially involved at any level. It was somewhat inevitable, therefore, that the cries of the VW racers would be drowned out by the voice of General Motors or Ford, who poured thousands of dollars into drag racing.

Dave Kawell and Jim Finch decided to move away from sedan drag racing when they built the amazing *Hot Sauce* buggy. The tube-chassis car ran well down into the tens thanks to a Kawell-built 2180cc normally-aspirated motor. (Dean Kirsten)

Throughout the heyday of VW drag racing at national level, the little Volkswagens won the hearts of spectators across America. Everybody appreciated the David and Goliath competitions that took place, enjoying the sight of large V8-engined machinery struggling to keep up with the tiny Bugs. There was a tremendous camaraderie between the Volkswagen drivers, with it being very common for one racer to lend his transmission to another if it meant that he could make it through to the next round of competition. Every VW racer has a story to tell of this unspoken friendship that set the Volkswagens apart from all others. They were special days that will never be repeated.

Bill Mitchell's controversial Motion Minicar-backed Bug put the cat among the west coast pigeons There was a lot of debate about the car's NHRA legality, but eventually this first *Thunder Bug* was outlawed due to its laid-back windshield. (Hot VWs)

Larry Kelly crashed the Auto Haus Bug at Bug-In 6, the car rolling and eventually catching fire. Kelly is caught here at Carlsbad Raceway during one of the Drag Days. Carlsbad's facilities were very basic compared with those at OCIR. (Hot VWs)

Fortunately for the Volkswagen racers, there would always be alternative meetings for them to race at, including the DKP Drag Days held at Carlsbad Raceway near San Diego, the *Dune Buggies & Hot VWs* Drag Days at OCIR and, of course, the legendary Bug-Ins. Even today, there are many Volkswagen-only drag race meetings that give the Bug plenty of opportunity to flex its muscles. Still no other single make of car is looked after as well as the VW when it comes to racing.

Amongst all the hard work of preparing a humble Volkswagen to run in the elevens, the pain and suffering of crashes before people fully understood aerodynamics and the grief of major engine failures, there was plenty to smile about. In the late '60s and early '70s, Paul Schley (*Lightning Bug*) used to suffer terribly from nerves before a race, so much so that he came to rely on a bottle or two of Milk of Magnesia to settle his stomach. Another racer remembers with amusement how he would wander over to Schley and either lie about what times he had just run, or tell how Darrell Vittone had just reset the class record again. That would be sufficient to send Paul Schley off in search of his Milk of Magnesia. The next step was for someone to hide all the bottles he could find,

**Lee Leighton campaigned this beautifully-prepared sedan at the Bug-Ins. Car perfectly captures the style which gave rise to the California Look:** **bright, single-color paintwork, lowered front end, little chrome trim and the sought-after BRM wheels.** (Hot VWs)

bringing Schley out in beads of sweat as he shouted "I know you guys got 'em! Where are they?"

On another occasion, Ron Fleming was standing about 100 feet back from the start line when Paul Schley came to the line, having already been through his burnout routine to get the slicks nice and hot. As he sat waiting for the green light, Schley revved the motor up high when suddenly, 'Bang!' – through the decklid came a conrod which tore a hole in the bodywork and shot 60 feet in the air. It flew towards Fleming, hit the fence next to him and landed on the ground, having exited the engine complete with wrist pin.

Engine failures were a common occurrence in the early days as most components used were modified from stock. For example, there were no alternative conrods, save for Porsche 912 parts which had a habit of coming apart at the cap when subjected to high rpm. Crankshafts were largely welded and stroked Volkswagen forgings and

**One of the most successful VW gassers of the early 1970s was Doug Gordon's** *Underdog*, **a 1965 VW sedan driven by Ron Fleming (in foreground). Car ran to the NHRA I/Gas class rules, recording times in the low twelves.**
(Ron Fleming)

Two of the most successful drag race Bugs of all time, Tayco's *Madness* and the Bergs' family race car, seen here in competition at the NHRA Winternationals. Decals on bodywork were to attract contingency payouts.
(Hot VWs)

Rick Anderson (near lane) chases Dave Vanderbeke in the *Dyno-Soar* at Bug-In 10, April 1973. By now, the design of VW drag cars pretty much followed a set form: roof chop, lightweight fenders, spun aluminum wheels, wheelie bars.
(Jere Alhadeff)

cylinder heads were frequently just reworked VW dual-ports. As far as transmissions were concerned, most people ran with Porsche gearboxes because of the lack of suitable ratios available for VWs. Sadly, even the Porsche 'box, good as it was, could not always stand up to the brutal treatment at the hands of the VW racers.

The vast majority of drag race VWs started life as somebody's road car – *Inch Pincher I* and *Deano Dyno-Soar* being prime examples, as was Doug Gordon's *Underdog*. This started out as a daily driver with a 78mm x 92mm engine (2074cc). With a stock transmission, the orange sedan ran low thirteens while remaining street legal. However, one Friday night at Carl's drive-in in Anaheim, a bunch of friends sat talking with Gordon and decided there and then that the car should become a race car

forthwith. With that, they drove over to Gordon's house, took out all the sedan's windows, cut new ones from Plexiglass and then completely gutted the interior. The engine was stripped of its fan housing, and by Sunday morning, the *Underdog* was driven out to Lions drag strip, having been transformed from street car to racer almost literally overnight.

The first year the car ran at the Winternationals in 1969 Ron Fleming, who was driving at the time, found himself on the start line against Richard Bays in the *Little Giant Killer* Fiat. The *Underdog* had been running 12.20s while the Fiat was turning 12.35/12.40 most of the time. As Fleming brought the sedan into the staging beams, he drove a little too far forward and tried to reverse back behind the line. At that moment, the lights turned green and off shot Bays, leaving the *Underdog* stuck in reverse gear!

Bob McClure in *Little Leroy* (left lane) was one of the first people to successfully turbocharge a VW engine for drag racing, running low 10-second times at over 130mph. McClure (here running Lloyd Mosher) was killed in a flying accident. (Dean Kirsten)

Keith Longerot in *No Doz* fought long and hard to be the first to run a seven in a VW-powered vehicle, but it was not to be. Longerot usually preferred to run at the sand drags and is seen here making a relatively rare pass in Bug-In competition. (Rich Kimball)

The honor of the first 7-second pass fell to Dave Kawell. He got ever closer to the magic barrier using a VW transmission and then changed over to a two-speed Powerglide automatic. The result was the world's first sub-8-second VW quarter mile. (Rich Kimball)

**Chris Bubetz entered the record books by becoming the first person to run an 8-second quarter in a rear-engined sedan.**

**Performances were achieved thanks to a turbocharged, intercooled VW motor hooked up to a manual transmission.** (Author)

Volkswagen drag racing made tremendous advances in the 1970s and '80s, with records tumbling almost every season. The various landmark times of eleven, ten, nine, eight and even seven seconds have all been broken by Volkswagen-engined machines throughout the years, the latter by turbo-guru Dave Kawell in his dragster after a season-long battle with Keith Longerot over who would run the first seven. Kawell's time of 7.96secs/160mph, set in 1983, marked the beginning of a whole new era of VW drag racing in which turbocharged VWs were king of the hill – a point that had already been made to some degree in the late 1970s by *Little Leroy*, the amazing ten-second turbocharged sedan of Bob McClure. However, few barriers have caused such controversy as the matter of who ran the first ten-second quarter mile.

Back on the east coast of America, Bill Mitchell

of Motion Minicar was campaigning an outrageous-looking VW sedan by the name of *Thunderbug*. This radically chopped car stretched the NHRA rule book to the limits and caused a lot of consternation on the west coast when stories began to filter through of its record-setting ways. There was much talk of the car being underweight or the tracks being shorter than a full 1320 feet. Among the west coast racers, the people most likely to break into the tens at the time were the Schley brothers with their *Lightning Bug II*. Eventually, as the two cars came ever closer to racing head to head, Mitchell broke the barrier once and for all, running some high tens in late 1972. Almost immediately afterwards the Schleys followed suit to uphold the reputation of the California drag racers.

Probably the last great barrier as far as VW sedans are concerned was finally broken at the Phoenix Bug-O-Rama in November 1992, when Chris Bubetz ran an incredible 8.93 in his rear-engined Volkswagen Bug, complete with VW transmission. It is unlikely that any conventional sedan-style VW will ever run in the sevens – but, then, who in 1965 would have expected a Bug to run an eight?

# THE RACE CARS

## INCH PINCHER, TAR BABE, LIGHTNING BUG AND OTHERS: THE CARS THAT INSPIRED THE CALIFORNIA LOOK

No history of the California Look style of Volkswagen could be complete without taking a closer look at some of the front-running race cars of the day. After all, these cars were, by and large, the inspiration behind so many of the original fast street cars and their story is inexorably intertwined with that of the Look.

Undoubtedly the most famous - and inspirational - of all Volkswagen drag race vehicles was the *Inch Pincher* series of cars that came out of the EMPI empire. The first of these, and arguably the most well known, was a 1956 sedan, driven in its early life by Grand Prix driver Dan Gurney and then by Dean Lowry and Darrell Vittone, son of EMPI's founding father, Joe.

The car began life as Darrell's daily driver in the early '60s. It was a cherry red oval window Bug with a set of chrome wheels, sports muffler and a stock 36hp motor. At the time, his father not only ran the Economotors Volkswagen agency in Riverside, but also sold British motorcycles. Dan Gurney, who

**From little acorns... This is how the legendary *Inch Pincher* began life - as Darrell Vittone's daily driver 1956 sedan. Note the accessory bumper guards, the Type 2 wheels on the rear and the chrome Porsche-style rims on the front.** (Darrell Vittone)

**Top: In 1963 Joe Vittone teamed up with Dan Gurney, entering the '56 in the Grand Prix of Volkswagens in the Bahamas. Here, Dan Gurney is seen testing the Bug at Riverside raceway prior to heading off to Nassau - and victory.** (Darrell Vittone)

**The EMPI sedan returned to Nassau in 1964 but, despite crossing the line first, was excluded from the results on a technicality. Sitting** forlornly in the corner of EMPI's workshop, the *Inch Pincher* awaits its transformation into a drag racer. (Dean Lowry)

would later find fame as the head of the AAR/Eagle racing team, bought a BSA Gold Star from Joe Vittone, the sale marking the beginning of a relationship that was to lead to some interesting developments.

Vittone helped Gurney's motor racing career get off the ground, selling him a Porsche Speedster at a very preferential rate. Up until then Gurney, who had been brought up in Riverside, had worked in a factory. Vittone began to take an interest in the idea of competing in the Grand Prix of Volkswagens to be held down in Nassau. The Vittones jumped at the chance to get involved with someone with Gurney's talents, the intention being to promote EMPI's range of suspension products. The regulations for the event required that the vehicle remain essentially mechanically stock, and ultimately that would prove to be a stumbling block.

The car was rebuilt with EMPI's anti-roll bar and camber compensator and the 36hp engine was blueprinted for maximum efficiency. The only real performance modification was to add a sports exhaust system. Prior to the race in 1963, Gurney spent a lot of time testing the car at Riverside Raceway. This pre-event development gave the car the winning edge at that first event, despite Gurney being called into the pits after a few fast laps and asked to remove the non-standard tachometer!

When the following year's event came around, Gurney was asked to drive once more and the car prepared for another visit to Nassau. This time, there had been a rule change that allowed some mild engine work to be carried out. Dean Lowry, by then working with Vittone at the EMPI shop, took time to port and polish the stock heads, shim up the valve springs and hopefully give the little sedan some extra pep.

The car proved to be too quick as far as the officials were concerned and, despite it crossing the line first, they disqualified Gurney for running non-stock valve springs. The victor's laurels went instead to the second place man, none other than AJ Foyt, later to become the hero of the Indianapolis 500.

The whole episode left a bad taste in Vittone's mouth and his interests turned elsewhere. The car was returned to its former role as Darrell's daily

The photo is from 1966, the event is the *Hot Rod* Meet at Riverside Raceway, just down the street from EMPI's headquarters. Dean Lowry looks suitably pleased, having won the class championship. Note the Rader wheels fitted to the Bug. (Dean Lowry)

1965 at Riverside. Slogans on the decklid were jibes at owners of Chevrolets ("Blue Flamers") and Ford ("Flatheads"). Bright red paint of old had been brightened up by the addition of a pair of racing stripes in white. Car was still street legal. (Dean Lowry)

driver, but not for long. Dean Lowry, keen for EMPI to become involved with drag racing, built a 1700cc version of the 36hp engine, slipped it into the red '56 and took it to the strip. With gutted interior, the car ran well against its class opponents which comprised Hudsons, Ford Flatheads and other much bigger machinery.

By September 1964 the car had run as quick as 14.90secs/91.5mph at Pomona with Darrell Vittone at the wheel. In February of the following year, at the NHRA Winternationals, the car, by now dubbed *Inch Pincher* because of its ability to win despite a lack of cubic inches, was quickest in its class with a 14.79, but sadly a string of transmission breakages kept it from making the record books. It was then that the *Inch Pincher* finally made the transition from street'n'strip car to out-and-out race vehicle.

At that time the car was running Denzel heads on the 36hp-based engine with a pair of Solex 40P11 carburetors, complete with velocity stacks from an old Porsche Super 90, supplying the fuel. This combination was good enough for the car to run down into the 13-second bracket. The next stage in the car's development happened when Darrell was called into the army and it passed into the care of Dean Lowry. The Denzel–equipped 36hp engine was swapped for a 1900cc 40hp-based unit equipped with a pair of Okrasa heads and dual 48IDA Webers. It ran in that same basic configuration until late in 1967, by which time Volkswagen's own dual-port cylinder heads were about to become available. As a true measure of the car's performance potential, Lowry ran *Inch Pincher* at the Riverside ½mile drags in April 1966. With an elapsed time of 22.04 seconds, the terminal speed proved to be some 115.5mph. When Lowry went to collect the timing ticket after the first pass, Jim Lindsay in charge of timing control told him that he

**Interior view of the '56 shows Nardi steering wheel, gauges for oil pressure and temperature and a tachometer - the latter had to be removed during the 1963 race because the officials felt it gave Dan Gurney an unfair advantage over the other drivers!**
(Darrell Vittone)

**The engine for Gurney's race-winning car was nothing out of the ordinary as the regulations only allowed minor modifications. Velocity stack on a stock carburetor, equal-length exhaust headers and a Bosch 010 distributor are the obvious changes.**
(Darrell Vittone)

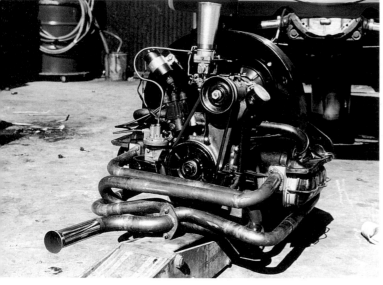

didn't have one. After the second pass, also 115mph, Lindsay gave him the first ticket and said "I didn't want to give it to you at first because I didn't believe a Volkswagen could go that fast!"

The one major deviation in mechanical specification during this time was when Lowry assembled a Shorrocks supercharged 1600cc engine fitted with a British SU carburetor, in spring 1966. The combination turned out an impressive 220bhp on EMPI's dynamometer and helped the car to record a best ET of 12.7secs/106mph at Carlsbad Raceway. Running on straight methanol, the car would provide plenty of crowd entertainment with its huge wheelstands on every pass.

That engine was eventually removed from the car

in 1967 and transferred to the ill-fated *Jouster* 'glass-bodied Bug sedan. The *Jouster* was very light, weighing in at only 500lbs with a four-speed Porsche transmission, but it was never a success. The car had a reputation, justified according to Dean Lowry, of being somewhat ill-handling. At one stage it was even fitted with a large diameter Porsche steering wheel to help Lowry keep it in a straight line. The car crashed at Orange County in 1968 when a Heim joint in the rear suspension broke as it went through the lights. This allowed the rear wheel to pull backwards and spin the car out. Fortunately driver Lee Leighton escaped unscathed.

*Inch Pincher* underwent major surgery in readiness for the 1967 season, when rule changes allowed cars in the NHRA H/Gas class to run to a 10lb per cubic inch weight break. The car went on a strict diet that saw the stock front suspension, floorpan, doors, fenders and front and rear deck lids removed. The original VW torsion bar front suspension was replaced with a straight axle set-up, while the floorpan was reskinned in aluminum. The original body panels were replaced with lightweight glassfiber parts.

Perhaps the most significant change as far as the look of the car was concerned was the removal of the original oval rear window section to make way for a later large rear window to both save weight and give the driver a better view out back. All glass was replaced with lightweight Plexiglass. The car was repainted in a period colour scheme of red Metalflake with flames and, for the first time, carried

1970, and *Inch Pincher* now sports a flower-power roof along with lightweight doors ( of the later large-window design) and fenders. The signwriting proclaims a power output of some 208hp, along with a list of EMPI components.
(Darrell Vittone)

In 1967 the task of driving *Inch Pincher* had been taken over by Darrell Vittone. This photograph shows how the car had by now been fitted with a larger rear window section to give better rear visibility while bracket racing. Note the "Sorry Bout That!" slogan.
(Dean Lowry)

the *Inch Pincher* name on the door. The rebuild saw the car drop to just 1200lbs in weight, a saving of around 500lbs!

Lowry left EMPI's employ to form Deano Dynosaurs with his brother Ken in 1968. *Inch Pincher* returned to the hands of Darrell Vittone, now back from the army, who continued to race it with considerable success, primarily in NHRA competition. The car was treated to a mild revamp that year, a patterned vinyl roof and new 'glass panels giving it a new lease of life. The fenders were now the later, upright headlamp style, while the rear decklid was replaced with one of EMPI's own, complete with the famous eyebrow scoops. The car was raced like this until 1970, powered by a 1952cc (88mm bore x 80mm stroke) engine hooked up to a Porsche transmission that was often to prove the weak link. With regular low 12 second timing tickets, the *Inch Pincher* became a feared competitor in the I/Gas ranks, setting numerous track and event records across the USA.

One particularly interesting aspect of the car is the choice of wheels throughout its life. In the beginning, a set of chrome Porsche steel wheels was used, these being replaced by a set of Rader steel and aluminum rims. When the legendary BRM magnesium wheels were released in 1966, the *Inch Pincher* was one of the first cars to be fitted with a set. Several photographs of the car at this time show it fitted with a set of BRMs quite unlike any other. Each of the five spokes is shaped, rather than flat as on the production wheels. No one is quite sure what the true story is behind these wheels: were they prototypes or simply regular BRMs lightened to save some precious weight? They certainly were not unique, as they can be seen again on an EMPI GTV car featured on the cover of the *1st Volkswagen Annual* published in Fall 1966.

As 1970 drew to a close, Vittone's thoughts turned to ways of improving the by now ageing race

**Now that's style! With an EMPI Imp Buggy in tow, the *Inch Pincher* was driven from meeting to meeting on this stretched single-cab VW pick-up. BRM wheels on the front have been painted red, while chrome rims are used on rear.**
(Darrell Vittone)

**For the 1971 season Darrell Vittone decided to build a new car, using the chassis of the original *Inch Pincher* fitted with a slick new roof-chopped body. The car ran unpainted for two meetings early that year, one being the NHRA Winternationals.**
(Darrell Vittone)

car. As the car was very much a publicity machine for EMPI, he felt that the old car had, to quote, "worn out its welcome. It had been around for so long, and everyone had become so used to it that even if I did do something pretty good, it would go by unnoticed". There was also the matter of ego. Again, in Vittone's own words, "Every time I went to the drags, people would say 'There's the car that Dean (Lowry) built' even though, after two years, there wasn't much of the same car left. That car was (originally) built by Dean and I wanted one built by me". He decided that the best course of action would be to start from the ground up and build a wholly new car - well, almost. He opted to retain the chassis and running gear of the original car, rebuilt and strengthened to overcome a few weak points, but to fit a new bodyshell. The original 'shell was sold, finding a new home in Mexico city.

The new body took the form of a chop-top '59 sedan that would take advantage of the new NHRA regulations which allowed a 4-inch roof chop in the gas classes. The 'shell was modified at the Economotors bodyshop, which operated in conjunction with Joe Vittone's VW agency, where it was chopped by 3⅞ inches so as to remain 100% class legal. It featured a Plexiglass "moon roof" while the doors, decklids and fenders were all replaced with EMPI 'glass parts that saved a whole lot of weight. The finishing touch was a set of polished BRM wheels.

The car ran for the first time at a small meeting just prior to the 1971 NHRA Winternationals, appearing in primer with simple EMPI logos on each door. *Inch Pincher Too*, as it was named, ran right on the national record of 12.11secs/111.5mph first time out. One week later, at Pomona, the car dipped into the elevens with a quickest of the meeting 11.98secs/111.1mph.

To record these times, the 1370lb Bug initially relied on an 88mm bore x 82mm stroke motor with an SPG roller crank assembly, dual 48IDA Webers, EMPI 851 camshaft and 1.4:1 ratio rocker arms and

**The car was sprayed by a painter called Molly from La Habra in a most outrageous asymmetrical design.** *Inch Pincher Too* **is shown here running at the 1972 Winternationals, where it defeated Ron Fleming in** *Underdog* **in the final.**
(NHRA)

39mm x 35.5mm ported heads. This was later upgraded to an 89mm x 82mm engine with an Engle F-32 cam and 42mm x 37.5mm heads by then EMPI employee, Fumio Fukaya. A 1⅜in header system exited through a chromed 28-inch stinger. On the EMPI dyno the 2-litre engine punched out around 170bhp. This was matched up to a Porsche transmission with a ZF limited-slip differential, chosen so as to make available a wider range of gear ratios. Despite a transmission girdle and solid mounts, this was always to remain the weakest link in the whole operation.

The car ran in NHRA competition only the once in primer before heading for the paintshop and being treated to what is undoubtedly the most outrageous paintjob ever seen on a race car. A mixture of Candy reds, oranges and blues, the asymmetrical design was applied by a painter known simply by the name of Molly in La Habra. Molly was a well-known artist at the time, painting dragsters and funny cars and dreaming up paint schemes for one of the major motorcycle importers.

The car was impressively finished throughout, with an anodized aluminum interior, polished wheels and plenty of chrome. Underneath the car was as shiny as the top, with plenty of gold cadmium detailing of both engine and transmission. Inside the car, even the roll bar was plated, while Vittone's wife Sharon stitched the upholstery for the seat and door panels. It was truly a vehicle that could have doubled as a show car at any time, very unusual in an era

when most race cars were definitely triumphs of function over form. The car's best ET was 11.5secs/115mph set at OCIR.

When Darrell Vittone left EMPI to start his own business, The Raceshop, with Dave Andrews and Fumio Fukaya in 1972, *Inch Pincher Too* became part of the deal in which EMPI was sold to Filter Dynamics, a large company that manufactured and sold automotive filters. It was driven from then on by Jim Carlson before eventually being sold to person, or persons, unknown. To this day, neither Vittone nor anyone else has any accurate idea of where the car is - or indeed if it is still in existence. The most likely fate was for it to have been sold to someone in South America, where it would almost certainly have been split up into parts, like so many of the other famous race cars of the era.

There was an *Inch Pincher III* - replica of the original *Inch Pincher* - which operated out of EMPI'S east coast operation, and also a replica of *Inch Pincher Too* run under the *NED Bug* banner by Denny Grove and Skip Hamm. Successful as they were, neither could capture the magic woven by the originals.

The EMPI race cars were not the only ones to become synonymous with fine detailing and superb presentation. *Tar Babe*, the VW gasser belonging to first Greg Aronson and then Ron Fleming, also gained an enviable reputation for its finish. It began life as a 1962 sedan purchased in 1971 in a stripped state for the purpose of building a race car.

*Inch Pincher Too* was finished to a very high standard, the paintwork being a mixture of Candy red, blue and orange over a white base coat. Polished BRM wheels added the finishing touch of glamor to this historic race car. (Hot VWs)

Even the underside was detailed with cadmium-plated parts and gloss black paint. Note the Porsche 4-speed transmission and the traction bar under the rear of engine. Small aluminum fuel tank is located alongside transmission. (Hot VWs)

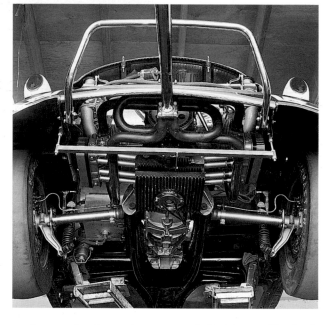

This photograph captures the superb finish of the paintwork on *Inch Pincher Too*. The glassfiber decklid is from EMPI. Scoops on the sides helped to channel air into the engine bay. Where did this car end up? Nobody seems to know. (Hot VWs)

The bodyshell was sent directly over to Leonard Becker's Bug House on Lincoln Avenue, Orange, where it was to be roof-chopped in readiness for NHRA competition. Most VW race cars at that time were pretty much hacked and stripped, in Aronson's eyes, and what he was after was a car that would stand close scrutiny in the pit area. The project took a long time to reach fruition at Becker's as it was largely worked on in spare time – Aronson would drive over to the bodyshop after work to help Leonard Becker with the bodywork and gently encourage him to get the roof chop done.

At first the top was chopped the legal 4 inches maximum but, rather than follow the usual method of cutting the roof into four or more pieces to allow the pillars to line up, the whole windshield and cowl panel was moved back. Unfortunately, when this work was all but completed, the NHRA released details of some rule changes. Amongst these was a note stating that the windshield could not be moved

Car and trailer broke loose on the way to the 1971 NHRA meeting at Indy but the car was repaired sufficiently for it to win its class that weekend. Not an auspicious way to start your weekend's racing, but at least it eventually came good! (Darrell Vittone)

Skipp Hamm and Denny Grove campaigned this eastern version of *Inch Pincher Too* under the *NED Bug II* title. Grove drove the car to victory in H/Gas at the 1972 NHRA Winternationals, beating the Schley brothers in the process. (NHRA)

from its original position – it was still OK to chop the top, but not to lay the windshield back or otherwise move it. This rule change was to affect more than one VW racer across the USA.

The decision meant that the top chop had to be done all over again and that knocked the wind out of Becker's sails. This second chop necessitated the use of the roof from a second car to take into account the new cowl that had to be fitted. As Aronson had chosen to build the car to the I/Gas rules, there was no need to excessively lighten the body. As a result, all the body panels, with the exception of the glassfiber EMPI decklid, were the original steel parts.

Once the bodywork had finally been completed, it was prepped and sprayed in a flawless black lacquer with stylish lettering by Rick McPeak. The only trouble here was that McPeak mis-spelled the name of camshaft manufacturers, Engle, writing "Ingle" in its place on the left side of the car!

The car was finished in time for the end of the 1972 season and began a full-scale assault on the NHRA I/Gas class the following year. At the first event of the season, the 1973 Winternationals, *Tar Babe* succeeded in recording the quickest I/Gas time of the event, an 11.78secs blast at over 113mph.

The motivation behind these times took the form of a 2-litre 88mm x 82mm engine with the ubiquitous dual 48IDA Webers, Engle F-32 camshaft, Porsche conrods, 40mm x 35.5mm cylinder heads and a Vertex magneto. All the engine assembly work, including the cylinder head modifications, was carried out at Fleming & Aronson High Performance, the owner's VW speed shop in Anaheim.

When the car was first conceived, very little was known about aerodynamics, but gradually more and more VW drag racers came to appreciate the dangers of having air pass underneath a car, especially when travelling at high speed. Already a number of well–

**The NHRA class rules required that each vehicle be fitted with functional headlights, but that didn't mean they had to be the original headlights! Small motorcycle type units were popular as they saved weight yet fitted the letter of the law.** (Greg Bunch)

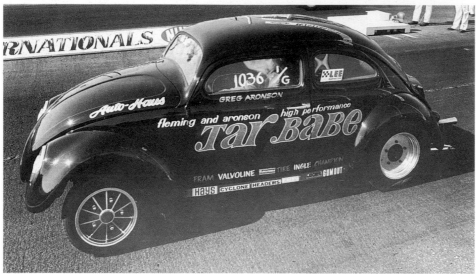

**In the first round of I/Gas at the 1973 Winternationals, Greg Aronson took the win as his opponent, Chuck Smithfield, red lit. In qualifying, Aronson recorded a pair of 11.63s and an 11.64, dropping to 11.82secs/112.50mph in competition.** (Jere Alhadeff)

known racers had suffered major accidents – notably Paul Schley in *Lightning Bug* and Dean Lowry in *Deano Dyno-Soar* – so Aronson set out to make the new car as stable as possible. When first built, it featured 125-section Pirelli tyres on BRM wheels on the front matched by another pair of BRMs on the back, these being shod with M&H Racemaster slicks. At a later stage the front wheels were swapped for some Mitchell spindle-mount rims to which Aronson fitted a pair of low-profile Formula Vee-style tires. These, when used in conjunction with a pair of home-brewed lowered spindles, had the effect of reducing the ride height considerably. A Porsche transmission was fitted at the same time to replace the original VW unit.

Everything was fine until the first run one Wednesday evening at Orange County Raceway. As the car passed through the timing light on deceleration, the right hand tire touched the front fender because the car was so low. This had the effect of locking up one front wheel and causing the car to turn violently to one side, spin through 360°, cross over the track, get up on two wheels and hit the guard rail in the right hand lane with the back end. The EMPI decklid flew 50 feet through the air and the whole car was badly damaged.

After all the hard work that he had put into the car, Greg Aronson felt understandably deflated. He loaded the car back onto the trailer and, in his own words, "pretty much decided there and then to pack it all in". At this point, Ron Fleming, Aronson's partner, offered to buy the car for $12,000 and so it began a new life.

Fleming campaigned the rebuilt *Tar Babe* for a further three or four months, running a best time of 11.53 until he had an offer from Darrell Vittone to race the car in Mexico City in 1973. A promoter there had offered to pay Ron $1000 tow money and a further $1000 appearance money if he would take the car, which was more than enough to tempt him. He enlisted the help of Greg Aronson and Mike Hunsaker and trailered the race car all the way south of the border.

At his first attempt to run *Tar Babe*, Fleming was beaten by a local car for the simple reason that he had neglected to alter the carburetor jetting to take into account the higher altitude – some 7,000 feet above sea level – of the Mexican track. Once that had been taken care of, *Tar Babe* returned to its winning ways. The car attracted a lot of attention and eventually Fleming was asked if he wanted to sell it. A price of some $20,000 was agreed upon.

**Greg Aronson's** *Tar Babe* **was without doubt one of the best-looking race cars ever built. With a flawless roof-chop, high-gloss black lacquer and stylish signwriting (even if the artist did spell Engle with an 'I'!),** *Tar Babe* **was impressive.**
(Jere Alhadeff)

*Tar Babe***'s roof-chop, neatly executed by Leonard Becker, had to be done twice as the first effort would not have been legal under newly introduced NHRA regulations, which stated that the windshield angle must remain stock.**
(Jere Alhadeff)

Sadly, *Tar Babe* was broken up, with the bodyshell going to one racer, the engine to another, the trans to a third, etc. So, like several other race cars before it and many since, *Tar Babe* disappeared into Volkswagen legend, leaving behind it an image of lasting beauty.

The name *Lightning Bug* used to be guaranteed to strike terror into the hearts of many an opponent in both NHRA and regular VW competition. Run by the Schley brothers, Mark and Paul, the two *Lightning Bug* sedans and the *Lightning Bug* dragster were heavy hitters on the race scene throughout the mid- to late-'70s.

The Schleys became interested in VWs as a result of their uncle, who ran a succession of Bugs, starting with a brand new '55 sedan, followed by a '59. The two brothers used to laugh at the funny looking cars and, being brought up in southern California, found more to interest them in the world of Chevies, Fords, Chryslers and other high horsepower cars that could go fast. In late '62 they began to look into buying a car for themselves and were down at a Pontiac dealership in Newport Beach when a Bug convertible, complete with four or five girls on board, drove past. The salesman pointed to the VW and suggested that this was the kind of car the Schleys should buy if they wanted to be popular with the girls!

They heeded the suggestion and shortly after visited Chuck Iverson VW in Newport Beach

The Schley brothers, Paul and Mark, stand next to their first VW, a 1963 sedan bought new from Chuck Iverson in Newport Beach. A visit to Dean Lowry at EMPI soon saw the brothers on the road to drag race success. Best time, 19.70. (Schley brothers)

The Schleys began building the replacement in December 1969, deciding to acid dip the body to save weight. Unfortunately they became engrossed in a football game and left the 'shell in the tank for too long, with dire consequences.
(Schley brothers)

Lowry persuaded the Schleys that if they wished to race properly they would have to build a race car. They bought an old 1953 VW which they proceeded to strip out and convert into the *Lightning Bug*. Car was destroyed at Bug-In 3.
(Schley Brothers)

where they purchased a brand new black 1963 sedan which they had fitted with an EMPI camber compensator and a set of chrome wheels with fake knock-off hubs. They bought the car on the Friday and returned on the Monday for the first 500 mile service, having put most of those miles on the car the first evening! Costing them $52 a month, the black Bug became their regular transport while their friends were all driving 409 Chevrolets and other muscle cars.

They visited Jardine Headers and had them make up a more efficient exhaust system after reading Henry Elfrink's book *All About Volkswagens* which offered advice on performance tuning the Bug. In December 1963 they read an article in the *Los Angeles Times* about a Volkswagen from Riverside that was capable of running at just under 100mph on the drag strip, driven by a Dean Lowry. The car was, of course, the original *Inch Pincher*.

They drove across to meet Dean Lowry and Darrell Vittone, who was still at high school just like the Schleys. They primarily went to see the car that

The new *Lightning Bug* appeared just 19 days after the project got under way. It appeared in primer at the 1970 Winternationals where it ran a class best of 12.35. Car was sidelined after the Schleys loaned transmission to Dean Lowry. (NHRA)

Dan Gurney had been driving in the Nassau Grand Prix, Gurney being a local resident to them in Costa Mesa at this time. Lowry talked with them at length and gave them a catalog which they took away and virtually memorized.

Over the course of their next few return visits, the Schleys became firm friends with Dean Lowry and eventually purchased a Shorrocks-supercharged engine that he had built at EMPI and used in the original *Inch Pincher*. Lowry educated the two on the facts of life about running any performance engine, explaining to them at length how important regular maintenance was for reliability. They put the new engine in the black sedan and took it out to Lions drag strip where they had a lot of fun, running a best time of 19.70secs/62mph. As the car was now almost a race vehicle, they decided to give it a name. The two brothers were beginning to lose their hair, so they called the Bug the *Hairless Beetle*! However, it wasn't long before Dean Lowry suggested that, if they wanted to go racing properly, they should build themselves a race car, not play with their road car.

As a result, the two went out and bought an old '53 VW to use as a base for their first race car. They fitted a Porsche transmission and refitted the stock engine in their street car, slipping the supercharged engine into the race car. With this combination, the car ran a best of 16.01 seconds for the quarter mile. Lowry let them into a lot of secrets that he had learned from running *Inch Pincher* and then built

them a dual 48IDA 1600cc engine, with dual port heads, 78mm crankshaft, 83mm cylinders, cut and welded high-lift rocker arms, which produced more horsepower than he or anyone at EMPI had seen from such a small motor. Once again, Lowry impressed on them the importance of regular maintenance, telling them to their horror how they would need to change the rod bearings every ten passes if the engine was to live.

The car was raced for about two months without any name and ran consistent high 14s. A sponsorship deal with Don Burns Volkswagen lasted approximately a year, during which time the name *Lightning Bug* was decided upon. By the end of their tie up with Don Burns, the '53 had run regular high 12s. Sponsorship from EMPI then followed and the Schleys built the first engine of their own. This 78mm x 85.5mm motor saw the *Lightning Bug* running regular 12.50s at 106mph, collecting two national records on the way.

The two brothers shared the driving of the car, but were aware of the problems this would create in terms of consistency. In the end, they agreed to each drive the car for two months at a time. However, on that fateful day at Bug-In 3 in 1969, Mark took the wheel in place of Paul and suffered one of the worst accidents ever seen at Orange County (described later in the chapter on the Bug-Ins). The resultant destruction of *Lightning Bug* made the brothers decide to retire from racing. They began stripping the remains of the original *Lightning Bug* just three days after the crash.

However, any plans for retirement lasted just two months before the Schleys began mapping out a new race car. They actually built the replacement in just 19 days, ready for the 1970 Winternationals at Pomona. The car appeared there in primer with an assortment of body panels in varying shades, but still proudly bearing the new name - *Lightning Bug II* - handwritten on both doors.

There is an amusing story about the new car involving an attempt to lighten the bodyshell as much as possible. The brothers had acquired another oval window body which they decided to have dipped in acid. However, being short of money, as usual, they called on the services of an inexpensive acid-dipper whose tank could only take half the 'shell at a time. Unfortunately, the day they chose to carry out the operation - January 1st 1970 - happened to coincide with the Rose Bowl football game. One end of the bodyshell was suspended in the acid tank and the crew left to watch the game on TV. At half time, they came back to turn the body round and dip the other end. Unfortunately, at that point, they became so engrossed in the football they forgot the bodyshell, only to discover later that

the acid had eaten its way through the metal! Needless to say, the 'shell was scrap.

The new car was a 1960 sedan which appeared initially with a full-height roof. It was built up on a 1958 chassis and featured many tricks learnt from the original *Lightning Bug* and, as a result, proved to be a vastly superior car. The body and chassis were both acid-dipped (this time a football game wasn't allowed to interrupt proceedings!) and aluminum inserts in the floorpan helped to keep the weight down further. The bodyshell was lightened with the addition of EMPI 'glass fenders, doors and decklids laid up by Don Roundtree. Once assembled, the body was treated to a coat of Candy blue pearl by Don Kirby and the characteristic zig-zag *Lightning Bug* graphics were then added to complete the picture.

As suspension failure was thought to be the cause of the accident that saw the original *Lightning Bug* destroyed, the VW torsion bar assembly was replaced by a DDS tube axle arrangement on the new car. Wheels were spun aluminum ET mags while rear tires were usually 6.60x15 M&H slicks. To power the vehicle down the track, a 2180cc engine was built by Paul Schley using an 82mm Okrasa crankshaft with 92mm NPR cylinders, Porsche conrods and an EMPI camshaft and valve train. With dual 48IDA Webers and reworked 46mm x 39mm valves - huge by 1972 standards - the engine pushed the 1080lb car down the track in the high tens.

The car was raced in this configuration for a short while until the brothers decided to chop the roof so as to lose weight and gain an aerodynamic

At the 1972 Winternationals *Lightning Bug II* appeared with its full roof-chop for the first time. In the final against Denny Grove, Paul Schley missed the first-to-second gear shift and handed the H/Gas win to the Skip Hamm's *NED-Bug II*. (NHRA)

**Despite the addition of wheelie bars, the front-running gassers were still capable of lifting the front wheels two feet in the air if track conditions were right. Paul Schley demonstrates this ability while testing at Orange County!** (Jere Alhadeff)

**Unusual angle of *Lightning Bug II* shows the Plexiglass roof insert used to save weight. The car was very well prepared and looked attractive in its blue paintwork with gold leaf lettering. Pinstriping was in vogue in the '70s.** (Author)

advantage. *Lightning Bug* continued to compete all over the USA, the Schley brothers' entourage – the team had a reputation for being one of the largest in VW circles – eventually covering 120,000 miles in three trips across the country. They were proud to have raced in 28 states of the Union and to have made many friends along the way.

However, in February 1973, the brothers sold their race car, having decided once again to retire from racing. As it turned out, after just two months away from the sport they felt the urge to go racing once again. At first the Schleys considered building a Karmann Ghia to run in H/Gas, but then reckoned that a full-on dragster would be a better route to take. Accordingly, a Type 4-powered, mid-engined rail was built and campaigned once again under the famous *Lightning Bug* banner. Although the Bug may have gone, the lightning still remained.

# THE BUG-INS

## THE STORY OF THE LARGEST OF ALL CALIFORNIAN VOLKSWAGEN EVENTS WHICH BECAME THE FOCUS OF THE VW SCENE

*Why a Bug-In? Well, to those of you who've been very close to the buggy scene for some time, it seems that all of the organized activities have been either off-road races, such as the forthcoming Mexican 1000 race down the Baja peninsula. . . or for the duner who gathers his clan of buggy enthusiasts together for a day at Pismo Beach. . .*

So began the introduction by Tom Bates, then editor of *Dune Buggies* magazine, in the programme of the 1st National Bug-In held at Orange County International Raceway on Sunday October 20th 1968.

Indeed, until that point there had been no major events organized either for the street-driven buggy enthusiast or those interested in hot street Bugs. Today this may seem an unusual state of affairs, but it is true to say that the Southern California Volkswagen scene had always been dominated by off-road racing. However, by the late 1960s things were starting to change. People previously content to build very crude off-road machines for some inexpensive fun on the dunes of Glamis and Pismo were beginning to take a greater pride in their machinery. The gradual process of change began way back in the early part of the decade with the advent of the Meyers Manx and EMPI Imp 'glass-bodied buggies. These vehicles proved it was possible to have fun in the sand and look good doing so.

Pretty soon, some folk began to build buggies that were destined never to see the crest of a sand dune, preferring instead to roam the streets of Southern California in search of admiring glances

The Bug-Ins at Orange County International Raceway were the most successful VW events of all time. They grew to be the focal point of the whole movement, allowing the average enthusiast to experience the best the scene had to offer.
(Rich Kimball)

Vic Wilson was the entrepreneur behind the Bug-Ins. His background lay in the off-road racing scene, but he recognized that there was a need for a new type of event that would draw together every facet of the VW scene.
(Rich Kimball)

**The Bug-Ins proved to be immensely popular, with literally hundreds of cars waiting in line for the gates to open at every event. When camping was allowed, cars would arrive even earlier, some going so far as to arrive on the Friday!** (Rich Kimball)

from any interested onlookers. As time progressed there developed a spiritual rift between the serious duners and their street-driving counterparts. The latter didn't need to get their kicks by heading out to the boonies, while the former couldn't see the logic behind building an off-road machine that never saw anything other than tarmac use.

At the same time, the Volkswagen was making its mark in a big way on the American drag racing scene. With drivers like Dean Lowry at the wheel of EMPI's *Inch Pincher* terrorizing the Gas classes of the NHRA circuit, it was obvious to all that the Bug was a force to be reckoned with. Ironically, unless they went to an NHRA event, Volkswagen enthusiasts were all but denied the opportunity to witness the impressive performances of cars such as this. There were no race meetings solely devoted to the Volkswagen.

The Volkswagen performance industry was by now expanding at an incredible rate. Less than ten years previously it had been virtually impossible to purchase performance equipment across the counter of a speed shop. Now, with the advent of companies such as EMPI, Scat, DDS, and Auto Haus, the owner of any VW could readily buy parts that would transform the characteristics of his car. Not only did these freshly hopped up VWs find their way onto the drag strip, they soon became a familiar sight on the streets of southern California, too.

Although these various aspects of the Volkswagen scene were thriving, there was still no focal point to

bring the various elements together. Certainly *Dune Buggies* magazine (later to become *Dune Buggies & Hot VWs*) was doing its best to promote the whole Volkswagen scene but, unless readers could witness things for themselves, there was little likelihood of the scene expanding further. What was needed was an event to demonstrate to all and sundry exactly what was happening out there, an event where people could get involved and become part of the show.

Enter Vic Wilson. Vic was a very experienced and successful off-road racer who promoted off-road events under the title of Vic Wilson Enterprises. He recognized the need for a specialist event to draw together all the various facets of the VW scene and entered into discussions with *Dune Buggies* magazine. Fortunately Tom Bates, the editor, along with publisher Joseph Parkhurst, recognized the potential in such a gathering and gave the 1st National Bug-In their full support. In its December 1968 issue, *Dune Buggies* devoted a whole two pages to promoting the event.

At that first event the stars of the show were without doubt Darrell Vittone driving the EMPI *Inch Pincher* gasser, Dean Lowry at the wheel of *Deano Dyno-Soar* and Bruce Meyers' *Purple Potato Chip* Corvair-engined buggy. Together, these vehicles gave demonstrations of speed that kept the large crowd on its toes throughout the day. Who was fastest? Top speed honours went to the *Purple Potato Chip*, built by Bill Garvin of Meyers and Bud

The staging lanes at the Bug-Ins were always full of every kind of Volkswagen one could imagine, ranging from serious racers to everyday street cars. This photograph from Bug-In 8 gives a good indication of the event's popularity. (Hot VWs)

Bug-In 5, and hopeful racers line up to make their pass down the OCIR quarter mile. There were never any complaints about noise from neighbors for the simple reason that there weren't any houses nearby, just fields of asparagus. (Rich Kimball)

Whitmore of Crown Manufacturing, with an impressive 121.3mph terminal speed.

As with many of the subsequent Bug-Ins, drag racing was only part of the day's proceedings. Alongside the drag strip, an action-packed slalom event took place, as did some off-road competition, while elsewhere on the parking lot a full-on car show could be seen. For their $2 admission ticket spectators got to witness an impressive day's fun, Volkswagen style.

For Rich Kimball, soon to become the principal Bug-In organizer, this first event was something of an eye-opener. As an active member of the Newport Beach Volkswagen Club, Kimball attended a club meeting one evening where a fellow member brought this new event to his attention. Kimball offered to visit the organizer – Vic Wilson – to learn more of the meeting. He came away impressed with the proposed event and offered to distribute promotional flyers to help spread the word.

Returning to collect some more of these, he met the advertising director of *Dune Buggies* magazine, Alan Kuda, who was helping to sell advertising in the event program. As he had extensive personal knowledge of the local specialists, Rich Kimball offered to help out in return for a 15% commission on sales. The offer was accepted and so began his lengthy relationship with the Bug-Ins.

For the second event, scheduled for 16th March 1969, Vic Wilson called his new helper in advance and offered him the opportunity to become involved once more and, by the third event on 26th October that same year, Rich took full charge of advertising sales. By now the Bug-In had grown considerably in size and was therefore placing greater demands on the event infrastructure. Vic Wilson turned once again to Kimball and asked for some further assistance in the form of providing extra manpower. This was duly organized and took the form of six or seven friends helping out on the

day in return for free tickets. As the events grew further in size over the years, ever greater demands were placed on the staff in all areas of the show. What started out as an ambitious southern California event was starting to take on a national importance in the VW scene, with racers driving in from across the country to take part.

In 1970 Vic Wilson Enterprises expanded further, opening Saddleback Park, a large off-road facility close by that became home to regular motorcycle and short-course racing. Rich Kimball, although still attending high school and with marriage on his mind, began to work more closely with Wilson. He helped out at weekends and two afternoons each week before taking the plunge and working full-time. By Bug-In 7 he virtually ran the events with Wilson taking a back seat and in 1973 he assumed the position of general manager of the Bug-Ins, at the same time taking a more active role in the running of Saddleback Park.

Wilson's association with the off-road facility lasted until 1980 when it was sold. It was a deal from which Rich Kimball was expected to benefit but instead he made the decision to further develop the Volkswagen events at Orange County International Raceway. The result of this was the introduction of two more drag races - the Drag Days - into the calendar, alongside six off-road events. Periscope Productions, which ran the Bug-Ins until their demise, was founded in 1980 to take full responsibiltiy for the VW shows.

By the end of the Bug-In era - there were to be some 31 events in all - the original concept of a

relatively small VW-only show had grown out of all proportion. At its height, Bug-In boasted some 10,000 visitors and no fewer than 1000 competition entries. But if the events were so successful, why did they come to an end on 9th October, 1983? The answer was simple: the famous OCIR facility was scheduled to close later that month.

The drag strip was originally built in 1967 on land owned by the Irvine Estate, one of the largest land owners in Orange County. It was opened officially in September of that year by the son of Gloria Irvine and is thought to be the first genuine raceway park to be built in the country. OCIR was located just off the 5 (Santa Ana) Freeway, close to its

It is possible to get some idea of the popularity of the events from this photograph, which shows how jammed the stands became once the racing started. Doug Haydon leaves the line. Note the American Racing mag wheels on his sedan. (Rich Kimball)

junction with the 405 Freeway, and throughout its life played host to many of the top drag racers from across the United States. Sadly, the track fell foul of the property boom in the early 1980s, when it became obvious to the landowners that there was more money to be had by turning the land over to industrial use rather than allowing it to continue as a race track. The last drag race ever to be held at OCIR took place on 29th October 1983. Today, anyone driving south on the 5 Freeway near Irvine can look across to the left to see the offices of Priceco - this building stands approximately where the startline tower was located at OCIR.

With the demise of Orange County, Periscope Productions had little option but to draw a veil across the Bug-Ins. There simply was no suitable alternative site. By this time the majority of the southern California strips had been closed down for financial or political reasons. Fontana Drag City to the north had closed in 1972, Lions dragstrip disappeared that same year, Irwindale closed its doors in 1977 and Ontario Motor Speedway folded in 1980. The closest operational drag strip to OCIR was Carlsbad Raceway to the south, but the facilities there were poor in comparison to those Bug-In participants were used to. Unfortunately, the prestigious Pomona drag strip, which is operated by the National Hot Rod Association, drag racing's governing body, was not available as the NHRA was concerned that too much use of the track might result in it being shut down by the local authorities. Without a track, there could be no Bug-In.

For some reason the National Hot Rod

Association always seemed to look down its nose at the Bug-Ins, even though they were run at an NHRA sanctioned track using NHRA insurance and NHRA timing staff. The latter was a wise move as there were frequent problems with the timing equipment (including squirrels eating through the cables!) that provoked more than one complaint from various racers. However, despite the lack of enthusiasm from the NHRA, no other event held at OCIR ever came close to equalling the number of cars tech'd, qualified and raced in one day.

In the early days the NHRA's own announcer, Steve Crosby, was called in to handle the commentating chores, but eventually an outward-going individual by the name of Don Chamberlin was asked to take over. Don, a member of the Der Guteeneine VW Club, earned himself a reputation for being the loudest person in the crowd, yelling and screaming so that he could be heard even above the sound of full-on race engines. He was also an extremely knowledgeable VW enthusiast and racer, having competed since Bug-In 11 in 1973. He first competed in a Bug and then in one or other of the Type 3 Notchbacks for which he was to become famous.

With his non-stop heckling of startline officials and racers alike, Don earned the nickname of Dyno - he just kept powering on like a dynamo. Very soon he became known as the voice of Volkswagen, a title he carries to this day, and is warmly remembered by all as the man who was able to keep any event on its toes, even when the racing was at a standstill due to an oildown or inclement weather.

As with all events with a 15 year history, Bug-In has some tales to tell. Rich Kimball well remembers the problems he had with the event, as well as the good times. As far as major problems go, Bug-In had a pretty good record, the only exception being the almost disastrous Bug-In 30 which was at first hit by the threat of a rainstorm and then suffered the indignity of losing the timing clocks midway through the event. Understandably, Kimball remains none too impressed with the track owners as far as that particular episode was concerned. However, he is justifiably proud of the fact that, despite the size of the events, there were never any grounds for major insurance claims against the promoters or the track. Mind you, that is not to say that there were no accidents or disputes throughout Bug-In history.

One of the more amusing, yet potentially difficult, situations arose at one particular event where two men, whom Kimball describes as evidently coming from well south of the Mason-Dixon line, decided to push aside the only black father and son standing in line to use the washrooms. Around 50 spectators rushed to their aid and Kimball was called to sort out a commotion in the gents' washroom. When he arrived, he was confronted by the sight of a large black woman swinging her handbag at the two troublemakers, who in turn, took swings at the woman by way of defence. Eventually four helpers were rounded up and together they bodily carried the woman out of the washroom and kept her out of harm's way.

Kimball explained to the two men that their best option was to follow him out of the back door and across the track to the gate where they would be expected to leave. As they did so, Kimball turned to see a gang of people intent on revenge chasing after them. Fortunately, the sight and sound of VW drag racers waiting in line defused the situation before it could deteriorate any further!

Inevitably, with so many people crammed into the stands, there were occasional upsets but on the whole the events were good natured. By far the biggest problems were caused by the general party atmosphere at the Bug-Ins, where the heady mixture of alcohol and several thousand VW fanatics did at times prove a slightly volatile cocktail. Never was this more evident than when overnight camping was allowed at the track on the Saturday before the event. Kimball, indeed, describes it to this day as a nightmare, as there were more injuries and general chaos caused by allowing a relatively small number of people to sleep under canvas – or, more probably, in their cars – than by any other aspect of the event.

On more than one occasion, track officials looked on in horror as a good-natured bonfire party was turned into a potentially lethal situation when

**Rich Kimball, Bug-In organizer with Vic Wilson, always viewed the slalom as an accident waiting to happen. With speeds getting ever higher and crowds getting bigger, it was only a matter of time before someone would get hurt.** (Hot VWs)

**Larry Kelly decided to take up flying lessons while driving the Auto Haus-backed sedan at Bug-In 6. The car rolled and then caught fire, comprehensively destroying itself in the process. Fortunately, Kelly lived to fight another day.** (Rich Kimball)

**The worst accident of all happened at Bug-In 3 when Mark Schley crashed the *Lightning Bug*. The car flipped over the guard rail, having already rolled a number of times. Amazingly, Schley was not injured in this spectacular accident.** (Schley brothers)

someone threw a Volkswagen crankcase onto the fire. With their high magnesium content, these 'cases burned like a flare, much to everyone's amusement, but air-pockets within the castings would cause explosions that were terrifying at best, life-threatening at worst. In the cold light of dawn, it was not at all uncommon to discover the burned out remains of someone's Bug that had been parked too close to the bonfire.

There were never any complaints as far as local residents were concerned for the simple reason that there were no near neighbors. The nearest large body of people was to be found at the El Toro airbase, whose own jet aircraft caused far more noise pollution than any Volkswagen ever could. However,

on one occasion, a local farmer was left somewhat less than impressed by the antics of some Baja Bug drivers who insisted on turning donuts in his field of fresh asparagus. A bill of $300 was settled by Rich Kimball by way of compensation…

When it became clear that overnight camping was not a good idea, the gates were kept locked until 8.00am. The result was a regular traffic tailback for some three miles up the 5 Freeway. It soon became a challenge to local clubs to be the first into the track so as to be able to set up their display in the best possible position. Roger Grago of Der Kleiner Panzers Volkswagen Club recalls club members arriving earlier and earlier at the track, many sleeping in their cars outside in the entrance road, having arrived sometime during the Saturday evening. Having the best club display became a matter of honor among visiting clubs and to lose the best spot to a rival outfit was not something to take lightly.

Inter-club rivalry was to be responsible for one of the worst accidents to happen at a Bug-In, involving Roger Grago and his show-winning Karmann Ghia coupé. If having the best club display was a matter of honor, receiving the award for Most Represented Club was a top priority, proving as it did that your club was stronger than any other.

In order to qualify for the award, each club member was required to register his presence at the event, the total number of registrations indicating the number of members in attendance. At Bug-In 18, Grago, as club president, was proud of the fact

**Mike Smith became known as the wheelie king thanks to the wild startline antics of what used to be his road car. White '67 made the transition from being a California Look street VW to an out-and-out race car. It now resides in Japan.** (Rich Kimball)

**Pausing for directions at the gate, little did Roger Grago realize that later that day he would be driving home with the Best Of Show trophy on the back seat. Bug-In 20 was the event where it all came right for Grago following his accident.** (Roger Grago)

that there were more DKP members at the event than representatives of any other car club. Consequently, when it came to the awards ceremony, he was all set to accept the prestigious club trophy on behalf of Der Kleiner Panzers but was shocked to hear that the award was going to a rival club. To this day there is disagreement over the decision, although Rich Kimball maintains that, while there were probably more DKP members present, they had failed to sign the appropriate registration forms.

Grago, along with other club members, was furious. He argued long and hard with Kimball before storming off to his car. Each club member in turn pulled out of OCIR, ready to lay rubber all the way down the street in an impressive show of horsepower. Unfortunately for Grago, at the head of the line, things went very wrong. He powered out of the 90° bend at the end of the entrance road and accelerated hard in second gear but, as he shifted into third, the throttle stuck wide open. Ahead of

him were a VW Bus and a Bug, along with some pedestrians whom he was naturally intent on avoiding. The Ghia clipped the rear of the VW Bus and spun round, hitting, dead center, the one and only lighting pole for 200 yards.

The car was virtually destroyed, along with its driver. Performance guru Gene Berg and race driver John Preston were the first on the scene and together they managed to pull Grago from the wreckage. Keith Goss, whose own chop-top sedan had won the Best of Show honours at Bug-In 16, was following the Ghia at the time of the accident and clearly recalls seeing the driver lift bodily out of the seat at the moment of impact, being crushed against the steering wheel and consequently sustaining some horrific injuries. The subsequent demonstration of club solidarity is described in detail in a later chapter, but it is worthy of note that this, the worst Bug-In accident, at least in terms of personal injury, occurred outside the facility rather than on the drag strip.

**The car show was hotly contested, with more and more entries at each event. The show continued to increase in size to such an extent that it became very difficult to display vehicles to their best advantage, causing a few upsets.**
(Rich KImball)

**Judging the car show at Bug-In was not a task to take lightly. The judging team at Bug-In 16 included "Shaky Jake" (right center with beard) who was one of the best qualified to carry out the task, his own cars having been regular show winners.** (Hot VWs)

In drag racing terms, two of the most spectacular accidents occurred at Bug-Ins 3 and 6. The latter involved Larry Kelly "flying" the Auto Haus sedan, the car being destroyed in the crash and subsequent fire. At Bug-In 3 the Schley brothers, Mark and Paul, decided to see what their famous *Lightning Bug* could do over the quarter mile. Up until then, the car had always run – with considerable success – at NHRA events, recording times in the low eleven second bracket in H/Gas legal trim. The Schleys took a gamble by removing the roll-cage from the car in an effort to lose weight. Although Paul was due to drive the car, when the startline crew gave the signal to get into stage it was his brother Mark who jumped in and fired the car up.

Everything was going fine until the car approached the finish line, at which point it stepped to the right a little. Mark Schley realized he wasn't in a position to correct it too much and resigned himself to a gentle ride against the guard rail as the *Lightning Bug* slowed down. However, the car had other ideas and turned sharply left, sliding sideways on all four wheels. Schley sat in the Bug with his eyes closed, listening to the sound of tortured rubber when, all of a sudden, there was silence apart from the whistling of the wind as the car took off. Witnesses to the crash reported watching the Bug fly some 40 feet into the air, while Schley remembers the rushing wind followed by an enormous crash as the car returned to earth, landing upside down on top of the guard rail.

The roof was pushed down onto the driver, hitting him on the head and forcing him down into his seat. This action broke the seat mountings and tipped him backwards in the car, forcing him to lie trapped by the crumpled roof while the car continued its devastating journey up and over the return road, flying over another car as it did so. The noise inside the car was incredible, recalls Schley, who by this time was powerless to do anything about the situation. For brother Paul on the startline, it was the longest 60 seconds of his life as he raced down the track to discover whether Mark had survived so horrific an accident.

Unbelievably, Mark Schley escaped with cuts and bruises and today he attributes his survival to the fact that the roll cage had been removed. He feels

Car shows at later Bug-Ins were organized by Al Martinez of paint and bodywork fame. Al (center of the back row) was responsible for creating more than his fair share of show-winning paintjobs and is still involved with event organizing. (Rich Kimball)

that the way in which the car was damaged in the initial impact would have meant that, had the roll cage still been in place, the seat mountings would not have broken and he would have been crushed by the roof as it forced its way into the driver's seat.

Although never responsible for any bloodshed or serious damage, other than scraped fenders in the rush to get out, the car show was guaranteed to be a source of argument for a considerable time after each event. When it became clear that there was a great deal of prestige attached to winning one of the many classes at the event, Kimball took steps to make the judging as professional and fair as possible. He entrusted the task to three teams of six people, each and every car being judged by all three teams. An elaborate points structure evolved which was intended to do away with any possible dispute. However, human nature being what it is, the more complex the scoring system, the more complaints that arose. Eventually the organizers would have to spend up to an hour and a half after each event trying to explain to the losers why their cars hadn't won Best In Class, or Best Of Show.

Due to the restricted space available as the event outgrew the facility, a major source of complaint was the fact that show cars had to be crammed in like sardines. For many people this was no more than a minor inconvenience, but for others, who wished to show their cars with the wheels off and the undercarriage displayed to perfection, being squeezed into a single car plot was not a popular aspect of the Bug-Ins. However, to win the coveted Best Of Show award made up for any amount of

hardship, be it financial while building the car or spatial while displaying it. With the Best Of Show trophy went the title "America's Most Beautiful Volkswagen" and the most outrageous of trophies, the most prized of which today being those awarded at Bug-In 20. These took the form of half a Weber 48IDA carburetor mounted on a carved wood surround.

Until the arrival of one Larry Shaw on the scene, the show classes were usually won by cars that were the street-driven pride and joy of the owner. Shaw's car changed all that and is generally acknowledged as being the first of the purpose-built show cars. Displayed on mirrored tiles, with wheels removed so as to show off the fully-detailed brass- and chrome-plated suspension, the black 1962 Bug stopped the Bug-In 26 crowd in its tracks. The car remains unique in Bug-In history as it is the only vehicle ever to take the Best Of Show title three times ( at Bug-Ins 26, 28 and 29) as well as scooping class wins at many of the regular custom car shows that were a popular part of the southern California calendar. Interestingly enough, Larry Shaw earned himself a unique accolade, too, having been the only person ever to take overall wins in the drag racing (Competition Eliminator at Bug-In 24) and the car show. What makes the story even more remarkable is that the same engine was used in both the race car and Shaw's show Bug. That's a record that can never be beaten.

For many, Larry Shaw's Brass Bug, as it became known, marked the turning point in Volkswagen shows. No longer could a daily driver VW be

**The two-man engine pull contest saw some frantic action and proved to be very popular with the crowds. The Bug in the foreground is for sale, never raced, only used on Sundays for visits to local show, immaculately maintained, etc.** (Rich Kimball)

**The Best Of Show award given to Roger Grago was this fantastic trophy made from one half of a 48IDA Weber carburetor. Never again has any event organizer offered such impressive trophies as these unique creations.** (Author)

expected to win a trophy at a major event, the judges preferring to award points for extensive detailing and outstanding cleanliness rather than looks alone. To take this into account, a World Class was eventually instigated whereby the top show cars could battle it out for overall honors. With the car show held for the final eleven events under the critical eye of body and paint supremo, Al Martinez, anyone who took home the gold at a Bug-In knew he did indeed drive (or trailer!) the best of the best.

Aside from the drag racing and car show, the Bug-Ins also played host to some rather more unusual events, namely the slalom, engine pull and Bug-In Queen (and King) competitions. The slalom, a race against the clock round a course marked out with plastic cones or pylons was popular with the contestants, if not the crowd, but became something of a nightmare as far as the organizers were concerned. As speeds increased, Kimball regarded the slalom competition as a disaster waiting to happen and was none too upset about dropping it from the programme to allow more space for other events.

The engine pull was extremely popular with the

**Diane Severs of Merced was crowned Bug-In Queen at Bug-In 23. The Queen contest was always a popular part of the event - especially with the male members of the crowd, for some reason! As if the sight of several hundred VWs wasn't enough!** (Rich Kimball)

crowd and consisted of a two-man team having to remove and refit the motor from a Bug and then drive it across a finish line. The competition came to be dominated by Rand "Zubie" Foster – teamed with either Fred Simpson or Don Schenk – who eventually carried out the operation in just 2mins 33secs!

If the engine pull was popular, the beauty queen contest was easily the crowd favorite. At every event from Bug-In 1 to Bug-In 31, young bikini-clad ladies had the chance to win the title of Bug-In Queen. Eventually pressure was brought to bear on the promoters by the female members of the crowd who wished to have their own fun. The result was a Mr Bug-In beefcake contest, won, incidentally, on

**Larry Shaw's chrome-, brass- and gold-plated show car marked a turning point at the Bug-Ins. From the moment it was brought into the** **parking lot at Bug-In 26, no car show would ever be the same again. It won at Bug-Ins 28 and 29 too!** (Jere Alhadeff)

one occasion by announcer Dyno Don himself!

Throughout its 15 year life, the Bug-In earned itself the reputation of being the world's geatest VW event. While other event promoters might dispute that claim if it were to be made purely on attendance figures, few could argue that the Bug-Ins were the greatest in terms of race entries, action, quality and atmosphere. The Bug-Ins may have gone, but they certainly haven't been forgotten.

# THE CLUBS

## CALIFORNIA LOOK IS ABOUT MORE THAN JUST CARS - IT IS ABOUT A WHOLE WAY OF LIFE

From as early as the late 1950s clubs were formed to bring together Volkswagen enthusiasts from all over the United States. However, it wasn't until the mid-1960s that the club scene came of age with the formation of a significant number of Volkswagen clubs in the Los Angeles area. One of the first of these, Volkswagens Limited, grew to become the famous Der Kleiner Panzers Volkswagen Club and is dealt with in detail in the following chapter. By 1972 *Hot VWs* magazine listed no fewer than 100 Volkswagen clubs in California alone.

The majority of these clubs were for followers of one particular style, ranging from dune buggies to VW buses. Many of them were informal gatherings of off-road enthusiasts, who might meet two or three times a year at the dunes, while others were very formal in their hierarchy, with written constitutions, committees, presidents, vice-presidents, secretaries and other officers.

**Most clubs liked to put on a good display when they attended a show, and few made as big an effort as Der Kleiner Panzers. This display, at Bug-In 20, included the famous '63 ragtop of Jim Holmes (left foreground).** (Hot VWs)

In the 1960s there appeared to be an infatuation with Germanic-sounding names, giving rise to the formation of clubs with names like Der Volks Brückenaufbau, The Volks Chancellors and, of course, Der Kleiner Panzers. Later, these would be joined by Der Zöttig Kaffers (The Shaggy Beetles!), Der Selten Käfers (The Rare Beetles), Blitzwagen Association (Lightning Wagen Association), Der California Käfers, Der Eines Klub (The Number One Club), Der Winzig Wagens (The Tiny Wagens), Der Guteeneine (The Good Nine), Der Rennmeister Association (The Racemaster Association) and Der Renwagen Fuhrers (The Race Car Leaders), amongst many others.

**Also at Bug-In 20 were the members of Der Volks Brückenaufbau whose display centered around Frenchy De Houx's beautiful Karmann Ghia. This car took the Best Of Show honors next time around, at Bug-In 21 in October '78.** (Hot VWs)

Der Volks Brückenaufbau had its roots back in the late '60s with a group of VW enthusiasts, some of whom were members of the Volkswagens Unlimited Club of Los Angeles (not to be confused with Volkswagens Limited). It was in January 1970 that DVB was officially formed and, like many clubs of the time, its fortunes rose and fell.

Most of the problems suffered by DVB were shared by just about every other Volkswagen club of the time: when any new club is formed, there is always an all too brief period of enthusiasm, followed by a realization that only a relatively few members are actually shouldering the responsibility of running the club's affairs. Frequently, this would lead to a feeling of resentment, the inevitable arguments and resignations and, ultimately, the demise of the club. Fortunately, DVB weathered the storm of an unstable membership, eventually becoming one of the foremost clubs of the California Look era.

DVB met at a club house in Anaheim and offered membership to Volkswagen owners over the age of 18. Would-be members were required to attend five consecutive club meetings, their acceptance into membership being voted on by other club members at the fifth meeting. These were common requirements among VW clubs, although some others would waive the need to be a Volkswagen owner, offering associate membership under such circumstances.

In an effort to raise club funds, DVB organized a meeting at Lions Drag Strip in 1972, but that proved to be less of a success than hoped. Early in 1974 one

**Der Volks Brückenaufbau was a very active club in the mid- to late-'70s. The club name caused a few smiles amongst those who could understand the German language: it is a loose translation of "The People's Bridge Builders"!** (Hot VWs)

member suggested opening a roadside stand to sell fireworks in readiness for the 4th of July celebrations – this did prove to be a success, raising money for DVB to rent a new clubhouse and finance a 4-day winter break in the mountains! Later, a DVB Drag Day would be organized at Carlsbad Raceway or Irwindale on a semi-regular basis.

The club continued to flourish, organizing navigational rallies and caravans in association with other local VW organisations. A Top Ten was

This was the age of the Ghia, for the top show awards at Bug-Ins 19, 20 and 21 were all claimed by Karmann coupés (Jeff Benedict, Roger Grago and "Frenchy" De Houx, respectively). The engine detail on Frenchy's car was simple but flawless.
(Roger Grago)

Dave Rhoads is one of just a small handful of members of the City of Orange-based Der Renwagen Fuhrers members left in the Volkswagen scene. He still proudly wears his club jacket and displays the club decals at every opportunity.
(Stéphane Szantai)

established to take note of who had the fastest cars in the club, with the quickest running in the elevens and the slowest high thirteens on the quarter mile. Club fines were also imposed on members who failed to uphold the club's strict rules on behavior - anyone who repeatedly broke the rules and incurred regular fines would have a hard time justifying his place in the club.

The name, Der Volks Brückenaufbau, always caused a certain amount of embarrassment among the membership. When the club was first formed and a name discussed, someone in their infinite wisdom suggested what he believed to be the German for "The People's Superstructures". Everybody thought this sounded neat and so adopted it as the club's title. Unfortunately, a German tourist pointed out to them that Der Volks Brückenaufbau loosely translated as "The People's Bridge Builders"!

Der Renwagen Fuhrers was a club based in Orange with a clubhouse just off the Orange Circle, on Chapman to begin with, later moving to Glassell. It was a hard-core club where performance was everything, just like the original DKP. DRF always prided itself on having high-quality cars which were, in members' eyes, the equal of - or better than - those of the rival DKP. In 1972 there were 13 or 14 members, rising to a high of 22 a year or so later.

Prospective members would be approached about joining the club, rather than simply paying their dues and joining up. This way a strict control could be kept on the standard of cars in the club. The rivalry between Der Kleiner Panzers and Der Renwagen Fuhrers resulted in an occasional difference of opinion between friends and family. Mark Hunsaker opted to join DRF while his brother Mike became a member of DKP. Similarly Dave Rhoads, whose California Look sedan is featured elsewhere, became a DRF member after his neighbors joined DKP. The rivalry was friendly, but not without feeling.

A popular club activity was for DRF members to caravan out to Indio where they would then go

*Der Kleiner Panzers*
VOLKSWAGEN CLUB
ANAHEIM
THE NUMBER ONE VOLKSWAGEN CLUB
OF SOUTHERN CALIFORNIA
227 S. ANAHEIM BLVD. · ANAHEIM, CALIF.

MEETINGS EVERY TUESDAY - 7 P.M.
*Der Renwagen Fuhrer*
VOLKSWAGEN CLUB OF ORANGE
487 NO. GLASSELL 92666
MEMBER        PHONE

*Der Renwagen Fuhrers*
MEMBERSHIP CARD
I DAVE RHOADS am a certified member
of Der Renwagen Fuhrers Volkswagen Club;
promise to obey all rules and regulations there
DATE June 3, 1973
PRESIDENT Mike Dunphy
TREASURER Bob Chapman

cherry picking, just for the fun of it. On the way back, the cherries were more often than not thrown at other members' cars while cruising on the freeway! Other trips would take members to the Colorado River.

DRF always put on an impressive display at events, with banners and club regalia on show, along with trophies won by members at the various Drag Days and Bug-Ins. Some of these displays were elaborate, with hanging plants borrowed from a local nursery to add a splash of color to the cars on show. Of the 15 or so cars in the club, between eight and ten would be raced on a regular basis.

Many VW club members would participate in a number of local rallies, the most popular of which were the "dot" rallies. In the days when gas stations gave away free road maps, the club would round up as many as they could from the local Chevron station and punch holes in them. The punched-out dots of map would be posted onto a card and handed to each competitor who, with the aid of a complete map, would then have to try to find the

**Roger Grago began his VW career as a member of Der Guteeneine Volkswagen Association before joining DKP and has kept his club** **memorabilia in perfect condition until this day. London Fog was the favored label for club jackets.** (Author)

**Tongue-in-cheek handout telling people of a new "club"!** (Author)

BUG OWNERS !!

DURING WORLD WAR II THE GERMAN LUFTWAFFE POSSESSED A DIVE BOMBER CALLED "STUKA", WHICH WREAKED HAVOC ON THE FREE WORLD. THE "STUKA", WE BELIEVE, WAS LATER SHORTENED, WINGS REMOVED, A COUPLE OF WHEELS ADDED AND ITS NAME CHANGED TO VOLKSWAGEN. THUS, SO DISGUISED, WAS SENT TO AMERICA. (ONLY THE "HAVOC" REMAINING UNCHANGED.) JOIN THE "STUKA OWNERS AND PILOTS ASSOCIATION !!

STUKA OWNERS AND PILOTS ASSOCIATION

HAVE A HAVOC

DECAL

(TAX INCL.)

**The Valley Volks Klub operated out of the north Los Angeles area. The club style was very different from that of clubs such as DKP and DVB - note the panelled-in side windows. Bug-In 8 Queen hopeful, Rita Ledbetter, strikes a pose.** (Rich Kimball)

location of the punch marks. The winner would be the person who found each location while covering the shortest total distance.

These particular Saturday night rallies were organized by the Cypress Volkswagen Association and would take in a route that covered roads all the way from Cypress down to the hills of Palos Verdes. The total mileage would be in the region of a 100 miles or so. Other rallies that clubs took part in were frequently just simple navigational rallies that required the participants to decipher various clues that would lead them to a particular location, where the answer to a question would be found. Such rallies, which were organized by a variety of clubs, took place virtually every week throughout the summer months.

DRF began to go into decline in 1976, finally disappearing as an active club by 1979. In common with many other such organizations, the main reason for the demise of DRF was the increasing price and the lack of availability of good quality fuel. The first gas crisis of the early 1970s took its toll on the high-performance automotive scene as a whole, not just the Volkswagens - a situation from which the clubs never fully recovered. Chevron stopped producing their Custom high-octane (110 octane) gasoline in

1973 and it soon became necessary to start mixing race gas with regular to obtain a sufficiently high octane to allow a high-compression motor to live in a street car.

Several of the clubs were sponsored by local Volkswagen dealerships. In 1966 the Newport Beach Volkswagen Association (NBVA) benefited from the support of the Chuck Iverson VW agency. Among its members were future Bug-In organiser Rich Kimball, Lonnie Reed of the Head Shop (one of the many VW performance specialists in Orange County) and, at a slightly later date, Kris Klingaman, whose own fast street Bug would eventually become one of the most popular race cars of the Bug-Ins thanks to its wild wheelstands.

Most clubs had a distinctive look of their own as far as their cars were concerned. DKP and DRF favoured the smooth lines of the classic California Look, while a club by the name of Keep On Buggin' tended to attract cars with wide 'glass fenders, slot mags and whip aerials. NBVA members favored pinstriped bodywork as a distinctive touch. Jim "Shaky Jake" Babbitt was the most popular striper of the era, his own sedan having been a Bug-In Best Of Show winner (this was later followed by his "mobile toilet" Worst Of Show Bug which stopped spectators dead in their tracks!). Shaky Jake also carried out a lot of pinstriping for local VW dealers as well as designing much of the earlier Bug-In promotional material.

Many of the club activities weren't quite as legal as they might have been with - as has already been

Bug-In master of ceremonies and all-round good guy, Dyno Don Chamberlin was a member of Der Guteeneine also. Apart from commentating at the events, he also raced his famous Notchback on both strip and street.
(Jere Alhadeff)

Volks Chancellors President Craig Roberts raced his *Craig's Toy* sedan with considerable success in NHRA and Bug-In competition. The well-turned out Bug ran in the A/MC or A/MV class. This is action from Bug-In 11, October 1973.
(Jere Alhadeff)

reported – street racing being one of the more popular. Former Der Guteeneine (the name is a reference to the original nine members of the club) members Dyno Don Chamberlin and Roger Grago, later of DKP, recall being apprehended by the police having been caught racing on the street. Grago, who was working at Don Burns VW agency, was driving his 1700cc Karmann Ghia, while Chamberlin was at the wheel of his VW sedan. On a quiet street running alongside the agency, the two drivers decided to put each other's car to the test.

As the VWs sped away from the "line", a policeman by the name of Officer Morales drove past the end of the street and saw them. He promptly made a U-turn and drove back to apprehend Grago and Chamberlin. They were cited for Exhibition Of Speed, Speed Contest and Drag Racing On The Street – serious charges indeed. The two appeared separately in court and were able to prove to the jury's satisfaction that they weren't actually street racing at all. Dyno Don managed to do this by drawing a diagram on a blackboard which, by quoting the laws of parallax, suggested that the two cars were not actually side-by-side at the time they were spotted by the police officer, but some distance apart and could not, therefore, be

taking part in any kind of race. The jury believed the story and let him off the charge.

Grago was able to prove to the court that the police officer could not possibly have accurately seen what was going on in the small amount of time it took him to drive past the end of the street. Officer Morales had claimed that he had seen the two cars "stage", someone else drop a flag and the VWs race to the end of the road, all while he drove in heavy traffic on Harbor Boulevard. With the aid of photographs and diagrams Grago won his case and he too walked from the court without a conviction.

Orange County wasn't the only area to have its share of Volkswagen clubs. Both Der California Käfers and The Volks Chancellors were Los Angeles-based. The former was very heavily into traditional California Look sedans but the majority of its members lived in Torrance, Gardena, Carson or south Los Angeles. Feeling that the Orange County-based clubs were too far away, a small group of enthusiasts formed a club based in Gardena.

The club came into being in March 1975 and grew to have an active membership of around 25, with meetings held every Wednesday night. Membership cost $15 per year, which included a club T-shirt and decal. A club jacket could be purchased for another $15. DCK was open to owners of all kinds of VWs, including Ghias, Baja Bugs and buses, although by far the largest proportion of members drove California Look Bugs.

One interesting feature of DCK was the awarding of pin badges to members each month.

Kris Klingamann was a member of the Newport Beach Volkswagen Association and his race car did much to uphold the honor of the club. Other members included Lonnie Reed of the Head Shop and Bug-In organizer Rich Kimball..
(Author)

Fred Payne of the Volks Chancellors was a front-runner in the NHRA B/MC class, eventually setting the national record in 1976 with his colorful *Super Bee*. From 1973, Volks Chancellors became almost exclusively a drag racing club.
(Hot VWs)

These were for VW Of The Month for the most important car, Racer of the Month for the fastest at the drag races, Käfer Of The Month for the person who contributed most to the club and Navigator and Driver Of The Month for the best rally duo. Then there were a number of other not-so-sought after awards: Redneck Of The Month (?), A★★★hole Of The Month (for obvious reasons), Beater Of The Month' (for the person with the ugliest car) and Drunk Of The Month (for the most disruptive member at the club meetings).

Another club with a difference was the Los Angeles-based Volks Chancellors. This club was unique in being the only all-black Volkswagen club in the California Look and VW drag race scene. Founded as primarily a social VW club in the late 1960s, the Volks Chancellors didn't start out as an all-black club but most of its members happened to be from a predominantly black area of Los Angeles.

Members became very heavily involved with drag racing as the years progressed and came under the wing of Bill Taylor, whose Inglewood-based

company, Tayco, helped many of them to build strong-running cars. By 1973 the club was almost exclusively dedicated to racing. Fred Payne's *Super Bee* Bug was a contender for the national B/MC record while Ed Treadway and his *King Cobra* competed regularly in A/MC. Club President Craig Roberts, racing his *Craig's Toy*, was another front-running A/MC competitor. By the time Bug-In 13 came around in October 1974, the club was able to field no fewer than 15 cars in drag race competition. At that event, members came away with three wins, an impressive showing for just one club.

The Volkswagen club scene gradually died as the '70s came to a close and members grew up, got married or simply lost interest in VWs. However, some diehards have managed to keep the spirit of at least two of the original California Look clubs alive: Der Renwagen Fuhrers (Dave Rhoads and Roger Crawford refuse to allow the name to die!) and Der Kleiner Panzers. In fact, the story of DKP is so intertwined with the California Look that it deserves to be looked at in greater detail.

# DER KLEINER PANZERS

## THE 30 YEAR HISTORY OF THE ORANGE COUNTY VOLKSWAGEN CLUB THAT STARTED IT ALL

**Rare photograph of an early - possibly 1967 - club caravan to San Diego zoo. Caravans (club cruises) were a popular part of the DKP calendar.**

**Already a distinctive club style had emerged that set the DKP cars apart from the rest.**
(Greg Bunch)

The story of the most famous southern California Volkswagen club of all time, Der Kleiner Panzers, begins over 30 years ago. By the summer of 1964 a group of young, car-crazy college students had discovered the pleasures of owning a Volkswagen and formed themselves into a small club, Volkswagens Limited. The link between its members was simply a love of the VW Bug and the desire to spend time with like-minded people.

Amongst those early enthusiasts were John Lazenby, Pete Dayton, Gary Huggins, Jim Edmiston, Dwight Magill, Dick Herr and Brian Rennie who had met through high school. Lazenby had taken delivery of his first Volkswagen on July 31st 1963 - it was a red sunroof sedan to which he soon added a set of chrome wheels and Porsche hubcaps. Not far behind was a Judson supercharger to give the little 40hp motor some extra get up and go.

Volkswagens Limited gradually became more organized but remained very much just a social gathering. The first event these early members organized was a "caravan" from their home territory of Anaheim in Orange County up to Hollywood in March 1965. Magill's mother Sally worked for the Anaheim school system and allowed the club to use the duplicating facilities to print some handouts that were duly put under the windshield wiper of each and every Volkswagen the club came across.

That first event was a huge success, with as many as 70 cars - all VWs - parading across Los Angeles. John Lazenby remembers the excitement of cruising down Hollywood Boulevard and back on Sunset, driving two abreast with friend Rich Kugel. Kugel's own car was a gold '58 with a Jardine Headers logo on the rear fenders - typical of the pioneering California Look cars. The '58 was thought to be the best looking car in the club, its owner having a reputation for keeping it scrupulously clean.

A fine view of Jim Holmes's sedan showing the popular club style of painted rear brake drums, red line tires and a chrome-tipped megaphone muffler. The Holmes Bug was unusual in having a red racing stripe down each side.
(Greg Bunch)

A very early gathering of Der Kleiner Panzers cars at La Palma Park sometime around 1966 or 1967. Vehicles are all relatively stock in appearance. The stage in the background suggests this meeting was held as part of a larger event.
(Ron Fleming)

At first the club would meet at various members' homes as well as at Schneider Motors in Anaheim, a Volkswagen agency owned and run by Joe Schneider, a German ex-patriot who was to remain a friend of the club for many years. He sponsored the club and also carried out a lot of work on the members' cars, as a result of which many carried Schneider Motors licence plate surrounds.

By the end of 1965 new cars began to appear in the club, with Gary Huggins purchasing a new tan sunroof sedan, and as the club was starting to grow in size and structure a new name was discussed. After much debate the title Der Kleiner Panzers was decided upon in December of that year. It was felt that the Germanic-sounding name captured the spirit of the club, even if the German grammar left something to be desired. Roughly translated as the The Little Tanks (the Panzer being the most feared German tank in World War II) the name should strictly speaking read *Die Kleinen Panzers*.

Der Kleiner Panzers' membership continued to grow, with the arrival of Greg Bunch, Bob Sechi and Mike Touseo but at the same time others began to depart as marriage or the draft began to take their toll. Greg Bunch acquired his first Volkswagen in 1966 as a graduation present from his father. He had seen a few VWs running around Orange County but had never really shown too much interest in them until it came time to buy a car. His father decided that rather than buy one from a local dealership he would order it straight from Germany. Greg recalls the day he drove with his father down to Long Beach to collect the Bug and feeling slightly deflated when he saw the huge parking lot filled with hundreds of VWs fresh off the boat. Suddenly a VW didn't seem quite so unusual after all.

At college he saw a few other VWs that had been customized with wider wheels and Goodyear Blue Streak tires on the back. He gradually began to modify his own car by fitting a pair of Chevy 5½in rims grafted onto some VW centers to the rear. Through a friend who worked at Goodyear he bought a pair of Blue Steaks for these rims and then added a pair of Pirelli radials to the front. Tinted

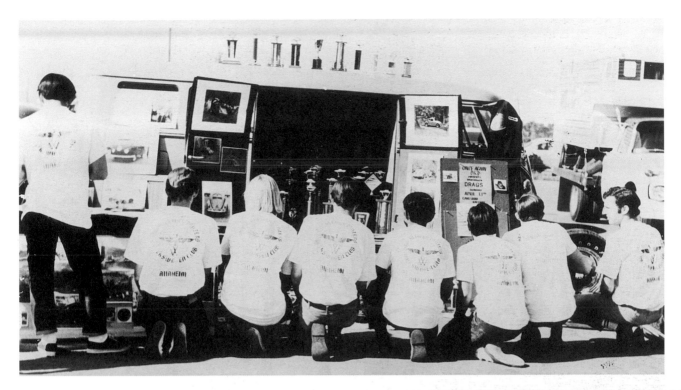

**A show of strength at a club rally. From left to right: Mike Bonilla (Banana), Mike Mahaffey (Howdy Doody), Ron Fleming, Jim Holmes, Bill**

**Aroyo (Wee Willie), Don Crane, Mike Hess, Mike Bennett (Ralph) with Rick Meisner's van.**
(Ron Fleming)

glass completed the look. The engine remained stock aside from a few chrome parts and an aluminium velocity stack on the original Solex carburetor.

While driving this car he met four other young VW owners, including John Lazenby and Pete Dayton, whose cars carried a decal of their club, Der Kleiner Panzers. They invited him along to Lazenby's house where they occasionally held a meeting. Bunch turned into the driveway and was immediately impressed by the quality of the cars he saw, each having a superb paintjob and being well presented. By early 1967 the DKP spirit had well and truly rubbed off on him and his car acquired dual Weber carburetors, an uprated camshaft and a Porsche clutch.

The membership continued to grow steadily. When Bunch was first introduced there were only 6-8 active members, but by the time he left to join the army a couple of years later it had increased to 25-30. Jim Edmiston, who had been one of the instigators of the club's success, left in February 1967 to join the army. When he returned in 1969 the emphasis had changed as Greg Aronson, Dave Dolan, Don Crane and Ron Fleming all became

**Dave Dolan poses proudly next to his "race car" - a mildly modified '67 that raced regularly at Lions Drag Strip. The Bug sports the prized**

**DKP Racing Team slogan on the decklid along with a "Caution - Race Car In Tow" warning.**
(Ron Fleming)

members and their interests lay heavily with drag racing and high-performance cars.

Dolan bought the chrome rims and Goodyear Blue Streak tires off Greg Bunch when he joined the Air Force and added them to his '67. The engine was modified, fitted with a two-barrel Holley carburetor and a performance exhaust system from Pat at Anchor Mufflers. Greg Aronson was

**DKP was one of the first clubs to issue rally plaques. If another club issued a quality dash plaque, then DKP members felt obliged to go one better. Plaques were affixed to the dashboard - the more plaques, the higher your standing.** (Author)

**Rick Meisner's split-screen Type 2 was used as the club display vehicle at rallies to show off the club's racing and show trophies. Note the** **club jackets on the ground (bottom left) and also the advertisement for DKP Drag Day at Carlsbad.** (Ron Fleming)

**Greg Bunch's original club membership card dated late 1966 and countersigned in early 1967. Visiting cards (top) were issued to members and were part of the elite image developed by Der Kleiner Panzers from the very beginning.** (Author)

progressively changing his '63 sunroof sedan, ultimately turning it into the first of the true California Look VWs. Don Crane bought a brand new red '67 Bug and immediately turned it into a street-legal race car, adding dual-port heads, 48IDA Webers and a set of BRM wheels. Across the decklid was painted the slogan 'DKP Racing Team'. Ron Fleming's black 1956 oval window sedan sported a set of ET mag wheels with Goodyear Blue Streak tires, a mildly modified motor and the DKP

trademark, an Anchor Mufflers exhaust system.

Between them, Bunch, Dolan, Crane, Edmiston, Fleming and Aronson began to bring about a change of emphasis in DKP. Whereas prior to their involvement it had been almost purely a social club, it soon became performance oriented. Along the way some of the original social members who had less of an interest in high performance were lost, but others with a passion for racing took their place. Gradually it came about that to qualify for membership of this increasingly elite club your car had to be highly tuned. However, at no time could anyone who simply owned a hot VW join DKP - the club had to approve of any prospective new member.

If a club representative happened to see a good-looking, well-modified Bug he would approach the owner to discover if he was interested in coming along to a couple of club meetings. The prospect would be expected to attend four meetings at the DKP clubroom and also participate in a number of other events over the next thirty days. At the end of that trial period, he would be asked to stand up and say why he wanted to join the club and then he would be sent outside while the existing members debated whether they wanted him in the club or not. A vote was always taken and at least 75% of members had to be in favor. Generally the voting was either almost 100% in favor or very heavily against. Rarely were there many mixed feelings.

Jim (Sarge) Edmiston's sedan had lost its bumpers by 1972. Car was nicknamed "Apalusa" by John Lazenby, its primered spots on an otherwise white car reminding him of the horse of the same name! Note lowered front end. (Ron Fleming)

Arnie Mohlman's '67 is a good example of a car under the Aronson influence: heavy rake, BRM wheels and dechromed bodywork all serve to give the sedan the unmistakable style of a classic California Look sedan. Photo taken in 1972. (Ron Fleming)

The hardest part of all was having to tell somebody why they hadn't been accepted into the membership. The most common reason was that their car wasn't up to scratch, but occasionally it would be simply that their face didn't really fit, and that was the most awkward news to break. If it was only a matter of the car not being to a high enough standard, then somebody like Ron Fleming would take them to one side and tell them what they needed to do to make the required grade.

What the DKP looked for most in a new member was dedication, not only to the club, but also to maintaining his car to a very high standard. It was not unknown for a member to have his decals scratched from the side windows if his VW had been involved in a minor accident. The decals would only be replaced once the damage had been repaired.

Club gatherings were held regularly at the Pickwick Hotel, where DKP rented a room, and always on a Sunday night - Friday night was kept for cruising (usually over to Select Autosales, opposite Carl's in Anaheim) and Saturday night was for going to watch a race meeting at Orange County or Lions drag strips. The club room was long and narrow with church-like pews down each side. It was decorated with club banners and the window at the front used to display the trophies won by racing members. Needless to say, it wasn't long before an impressive display of cups had built up. As the club evenings wore on, youthful exuberance would come to the fore and some members would hold an impromptu burn-out contest in the car park, much to the distress of the residents of the hotel!

With the club's new preoccupation with performance, it was inevitable that street racing would become one of the more regular unofficial events. A Top Ten ladder was kept at the clubhouse, consisting of a record of the fastest ten members' cars. Each of the ten would be capable of running the quarter mile in thirteen seconds or less, with another five or six cars all able to run within a second of that. By 1971 the majority of cars in the club ran large capacity motors with dual 48IDA Weber carburetors. Most cars were 1960s models,

**Another boisterous evening at the clubhouse by the Pickwick Hotel in Anaheim. Committee members Mike Johnson, Ron Fleming and Jerry Harmon join in the spirit of things while Craig Foster (right) looks less than impressed!**
(Ron Fleming)

**Pam Martin poses outside her parents' house next to Ron Fleming's '56 sedan. Pam later married DKP member Greg Bunch. Note DKP Racing Team logo, American Racing mag wheels and Goodyear bias-belted tires. A very clean car.**
(Ron Fleming)

but some, like Mike Mahaffey's or Bill Aroyo's 1951 split-window Bugs, were very much older. Mahaffey's Concorde Green version ran a 2180cc motor with Webers and was equipped with a set of BRM wheels, all guaranteed to make a vintage VW enthusiast red with rage.

Many of the clandestine displays of horsepower would take place behind the Nabisco factory or way out on La Palma Avenue where the road split into four lanes. Other popular areas included a street right by the Kimberley Clark factory or close to the original Carl's drive-in at a meat-packing plant. One street the racers used was about half a mile long and led up to a retail store. When the store was closed up for the night the street was empty, so somebody thought of painting start and finish lines on it to make things more fair!

Nobody ever believed that this racing was a good thing, but Ron Fleming recalls members being fairly responsible when it came to safety. Each vehicle almost always had seat belts fitted and just two cars at a time would race against one another. The chosen street would often be lit by the headlights of spectators' cars so as to allow the competitors to race in something other than pitch darkness. Frequently the police would break up these illicit races, on some occasions arriving in a helicopter equipped with a searchlight. That was the cue for everyone to dive into their cars and head off into the darkness.

Aside from the street races, a popular form of club entertainment was the navigational rallies. Virtually every VW club organized a rally of some

Roger Grago acquired this Karmann Ghia from his father in 1969, but it wasn't destined to stay stock for long. Pretty soon Grago fell under the spell of the California Look and the rest is history. Note German ADAC badge on front fender.
(Roger Grago)

**Enough to make a restorer squirm! Mike Mahaffey's (left) and Bill Aroyo's (right) 1951 split-window Bugs both sported BRM wheels.**

**Note the stinger exhaust tailpipe on Mahaffey's car. This was fitted for racing. Where are these cars now?**
(Ron Fleming)

kind, but Der Kleiner Panzers members went out of their way to make sure theirs were better than anyone else's. Theirs was the first club to give away professional-looking dash plaques at each rally and then, as soon as other clubs began to copy that idea, they made them ever more intricate. Each rally was given a name such as "Watch out, she's got curves" (a reference to the twisty nature of the route), "Deep Throat" (a play on dual Weber carburetors - well, maybe) or the more obvious "Takin' it to the streets again". There was a whole series of "Odyssey" rallies, too, with questions that could only be answered if the competitor had taken part in the previous rally.

The DKP members would attend events organized by other clubs and always made a point of caravanning to them in single file, the Top Ten club cars being at the front of the line. As they drew into the parking lot of somewhere like Montgomery

Ward, where many rallies started, each car in turn would do a burn-out to prove the point about DKP's obsession with horsepower. There was a lot of ritual attached to club outings and one was that nobody should ever be seen without their club jacket. These were simple maroon zip-front jackets, usually made by London Fog or Peters, which featured a patch on the back embroidered by a local lady by the name of Lucille. Try as she might, Lucille couldn't quite get the hang of embroidering a round patch, so they all turned out slightly oval in shape.

As the rallies grew in importance, so did other events such as the Carlsbad Drag Days and the Bug-Ins at Orange County Raceway. Der Kleiner Panzers was the first club to host its own drag race meetings, choosing the somewhat basic facilities at Carlsbad to the south of Orange County to hold them. The events were a great success, attracting up to 250 cars on more than one occasion, with the extrovert Ron Fleming acting as master of ceremonies.

At each of the Orange County Bug-Ins, an area was set aside for use by clubs to put on a show, with an award being presented for best club display. Naturally, Der Kleiner Panzers felt the need to outshine all the other participating clubs by building increasingly complex displays. To ensure they had the best spot at the event, some members would show up at the preceding Saturday night race meeting and wait until the car park had emptied. As the gates were closed, they would drive up and park by the entrance to make sure they were first in line the next day. When the Bug-In organizers made overnight camping available, some DKP members would turn up on the Friday night to claim a space!

Many of the members would race their VWs at the Bug-Ins, so an area would be cordoned off in

**Grago's Ghia was one of the first, and certainly one of the finest, of the California Look coupés. Gunmetal paintwork, EMPI GT (8-spoke) wheels and ground-hugging stance give this beautiful car an extremely purposeful look.**
(Roger Grago)

**Craig Foster was the owner of the first Type 3 in the club. With its panelled-in rear side windows, the Squareback had more than a touch of custom about it, yet remained very much a California Look VW. Wheels are EMPI GT Spyders.** (Hot VWs)

the pits and club banners raised to mark out DKP territory. At first, the club display would center round Rick "Mother" Meissner's VW bus, parked with its side doors open and decked out with club regalia. Then, when another club followed suit, DKP would build a more permanent display setting, eventually leading up to a two-tier set-up with viewing and hospitality areas, and food provided by wives and girlfriends.

The matter of girls being allowed into the club was a prickly one as far as some members were concerned, even though as early as 1966 there were at least two girls in Volkswagens Limited. Many felt that it should remain a male-only organization in line with Paragraph 8 of the amendments to the written club constitution: "No girls allowed in the club". Others thought differently and there were many heated debates on the subject. Several of the members did bring their wives along to events, but

Dave Dolan remembers one club meeting where someone jumped up on a table and screamed out "No f***ing chicks in the club!". A vote was eventually taken and girls were allowed in, but there were never many takers. As the club was not a social one in the true sense, most girls who did show an interest soon fell by the wayside.

The first chapter of Der Kleiner Panzers began drawing to a close in 1972 and, by the following year, it was all over. The whole club scene had started to diminish and for many, like Dave Dolan, who had been caught up in the draft, club life on their return seemed trivial. The armed forces had made men of them – or at least, instilled in them a sense that there was possibly more to life than, to quote a former DKP President, "Getting drunker than skunks at the car rallies and raising hell". Others grew out of their VWs, selling them to buy a Porsche, while those for whom the main draw was

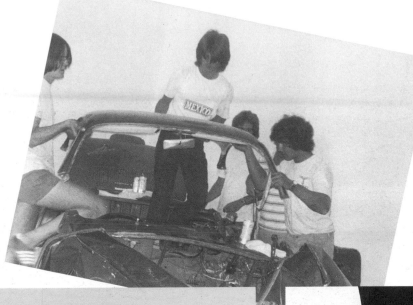

**At Bug-In 18 Grago crashed his Ghia into a lighting pole following a showdown with the organizer. Car was totalled and Grago badly injured, but club members ganged together and salvaged what they could from the wreck.** (Roger Grago)

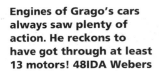

**The proudest day of his life. Grago (center in sunglasses) collected the trophy for Best Of Show at Bug-In 20 with his "new" Ghia built with the help of fellow club members. Display of club camaraderie was second to none.** (Roger Grago)

**Engines of Grago's cars always saw plenty of action. He reckons to have got through at least 13 motors! 48IDA Webers on short manifolds were used. Note Zolotone finish to engine bay - a popular paint treatment of the time.** (Roger Grago)

drag racing watched helplessly as, one by one, the southern California drag strips began to close.

The club remained inactive for some while, although many members continued to keep an active interest in Volkswagens. Some, like Ron Fleming and Greg Aronson, concentrated on building up their successful VW-related business. Others settled down to a more responsible family life and a career. None have ever denied that their period of membership in Der Kleiner Panzers was a special time in their lives. For many at the time the club was their whole life.

As the door was closing on the first chapter of Der Kleiner Panzers, some new faces began to appear on the Volkswagen scene, among them Roger Grago. He had taken a part-time job while going to college and his first recollection of the club had been in 1968 - actually on the very night that Richard Nixon was nominated for President. A

friend of his sister had a mildly modified Bug with chrome wheels and Grago went out cruising with him to Carl's on Harbor Boulevard in Anaheim. There he met a bunch of guys who turned out to be members of DKP. Among them were Doug Gordon and Ron Fleming who between them campaigned the *Underdog* race car. Gordon did a burnout out of the parking lot, chasing a Chevrolet Chevelle down the street. The display of horsepower impressed Grago, who was still too young to hold a licence, and he vowed that one day he too would have a VW like that.

His family moved to La Habra and he found a job washing cars at the Don Burns Volkswagen dealership in Anaheim. There he met a VW enthusiast called Brian Vaughn who belonged to Der Guteeneine VW Club which he duly joined. Working at the dealership brought him into contact with many of the local Volkswagen owners,

**In 1977 *Hot VWs* magazine arranged a photo shoot of DKP II members' cars in Silverado Park, Long Beach. Shown is Keith Goss's chop-top sedan flat towing Mike O'Neal's California Looker to the photo location.**
(Dean Kirsten)

**No fewer than 18 cars showed up for the *Hot VWs* feature, including the two chop-tops of Keith Goss (pale yellow, to the left) and Mike Martinez (black, to the right). The four Karmann Ghias included Roger Grago's (center right).**
(Hot VWs)

including several members of DKP. He owned a stock '62 Karmann Ghia which he had bought off his father, and knew nothing about how to make a VW go fast. At the time very few people had ever even considered working on a Karmann Ghia.

By the time Grago decided to leave Der Guteeneine, Der Kleiner Panzers had already wound down and, for a period of about a year, the club lay dormant. However, along with Randy Welch and Mike Dunfee (formerly of Der Renwagen Fuhrers), he felt that there was a need for a Volkswagen club that maintained the high standards of performance and presentation set by the original DKP. They were keen not to upset any of the members of the old

club and so met with Ron Fleming and others to canvas their opinion on starting up a second generation DKP. The majority of people they made contact with were more than happy for the club to start up again, although it would be fair to say that a few did express their dislike of the idea of the club being resurrected.

The trio began talking to others who shared their interest in getting the club together again. They started to have regular meetings at Mike Dunfee's house, and then at the Al Martinez body shop, and had decals made, just like the original club. Initially, the new DKP was harassed by some sceptical former members, but as soon as they saw the standard of cars that were being allowed into the club, the animosity gradually subsided. Indeed, Grago's own Ghia was one of the cars to be featured in the first California Look story in *Hot VWs* magazine, so gaining more credibility.

**Same place, different era. Silverado Park was the setting for another DKP photo shoot, just like the DKP II shoot in 1977. This time, the year was 1992 and the club is DKP III. The DKP motto remains the same: quality not quantity.**
(Stephane Szantai)

**Der Kleiner Panzers was always one step ahead of the other VW clubs when it came to self-promotion. T-shirts, jackets and flags are much sought after today. Club plaques, two of which are shown here, are the most cherished items of all.** (Author)

Membership grew until there were as many as 37 club cars at one point. Once again, high standards were maintained, with members being asked to cover up their decals if their car became scratched. The club held its first rally and that was a great success, and after the rallies came the street racing. Most of the cars in the club were very fast and many challenges were turned down by outsiders as the club's reputation spread. Roger Grago recalls cruising in convoy one night into a drive-in where the local Camaro club met and being asked if any of the VWs wanted to race. "Sure" he replied, "pick whichever one you want", such was the confidence in the VWs' performance capabilities. None of the

Camaros would take up the offer.

Grago's Karmann Ghia suffered its fair share of damage, mechanical and body. No less than thirteen engines were built for the car throughout its life as hard driving took its toll. However, it was at Bug-In 18 that fate took a hand and saw the car destroyed in a monumental accident which is described in detail in the earlier chapter on the Bug-In events. This lead to a show of club solidarity which remains unparalleled to this day.

Following the crash, Grago was loaded into an ambulance and driven to hospital but, while lying on the stretcher, all he could hear on either side of him was the roar from dual 48IDA carburetors as fellow club members escorted the ambulance to the Saddleback hospital. All the club waited in the reception area until the doctors decided that he was too badly injured for them to cope with and would have to be moved to another hospital. For a second time, Grago's ambulance was escorted by the rest of the club members. At least 15 members stayed until they eventually got thrown out by the medical staff and, over the next three weeks, Grago got constant visits from his friends in DKP.

While he lay in hospital, other club members had pooled together and bought him another '62 Karmann Ghia from Mike O'Neal. The Martinez family bodyshop donated a sizeable proportion of the paint and bodywork. Everything that could be

Randy Welch's sedan on the Freeway. By the mid-'70s, the club style was slightly less purist than before. Propped open decklid and buggy bar were new, but a lack of chrome trim and a bright, single-color paintjob were traditional DKP.
(Roger Grago)

Arnie Mohlman is unique in that he still owns his original DKP California Look sedan in very much its original form. It is seen here at the 1990 DKP Reunion gathering. BRM wheels and lack of chrome hark back to the old days.
(Ron Fleming)

salvaged from the original car was removed from the wreck and the new car built up to a sufficiently high standard to win best of show, less than a year later, at Bug-In 20. That was quite a day for Der Kleiner Panzers because club members took not only the Best Of Show award but also Top Eliminator in the drag racing and Most Represented Club. At that point, any doubts about the worthiness of the club to carry the hallowed DKP title should have been dispelled.

Following the meetings at Martinez's bodyshop, the club met at various pizza parlours before gaining use of a carpet warehouse in Fullerton. After a while the club decided to get its own club house, like the old days, and moved to an industrial area where they took over a pair of adjoining offices. The clubhouse remained until the demise of DKP II and each member had his own key so that he could go there whenever he wanted, for whatever reason.

The second generation Der Kleiner Panzers began to wind down in 1978/9 when the Volkswagen scene went into decline as the new mini-truck fad appeared on the horizon. The ever-increasing cost of gasoline and the shortages brought about by the gas crisis sealed the fate of DKP II and many other car clubs. Grago sold his Ghia at the end

of 1978 following his victory at Bug-In 20 and the club continued for approximately another year before it died for a second time.

History has a habit of repeating itself and, in 1990, a group of hard-core VW enthusiasts from Orange County began discussing the formation of a third-generation DKP. Bill Schwimmer, Dave Mason, Hector Bonilla and several others approached Ron Fleming to seek his blessing to re-form the club and, having reassured him of their high standards, went ahead. Their VWs capture the true spirit of Der Kleiner Panzers, with dual 48IDA Weber motors as the club standard, along with BRM wheels and the classic nose-down California Look stance.

Today the club is active, if not to the same degree as DKP I – but only because there are not so many opportunities. Members regularly attend the major VW events, putting on an impressive display of old school California Look cars that would have looked right at home at Orange County Raceway in 1970. Several of the members also compete in the Saturday night grudge racing at Terminal Island, proving that 11-, 12- and 13-second Volkswagens are alive and well on the streets of southern California.

# CALIFORNIA LOOK TODAY

## AFTER ALMOST A QUARTER OF A CENTURY, THE CALIFORNIA LOOK HAS SPREAD TO ALL FOUR CORNERS OF THE WORLD

**Larry Shaw's three-time Bug-In winner still looks good today with its brass and gold plating and black lacquer paint job. Shaw's car marked the turning point, bringing about the end of an era in which a daily-driver could win Best Of Show** (Author)

As the 1980s unfolded, the California Look style continued to develop, with an increasing emphasis put on creating cars with show-quality detailing throughout. The seeds of this new development were largely sown by Larry Shaw's Best Of Show winner, which made its appearance at Bug-In 26. From that point on, for any Volkswagen to win its class at an event, it would have to have been stripped down to the very last nut and bolt, detailed, chromed, painted and treated to any number of body modifications.

Shaw's was one of the last show cars that still had its roots set in California Look, but even this had crossed over to the full-custom style in some areas. Rear-hinged suicide doors, crushed velour interior trim and thousands of dollars worth of gold, brass and chrome plating impressed the judges, but not necessarily the purists. From that point on, there was a steady divergence of interests as the show cars went one way, the hard-core street machines another.

With the ever-increasing cost of gasoline, very quick street cars became thin on the ground for a while, but all that has changed as people have become increasingly nostalgic for the old days when cars like Greg Aronson's first made their mark. Nowhere else can this be seen more clearly than among the cars of the current incarnation of Der Kleiner Panzers.

**Bill Schwimmer, President of the third incarnation of Der Kleiner Panzers, runs this 1959 Coral Red ragtop sedan. Just like the cars of old, it sports a set of polished BRM wheels and a traditional California Look nose-down stance.**
(Author)

**The engine is a 2110cc "killer" with 82mm Gene Berg crankshaft, Carillo conrods, Cima 90.5mm cylinders and pistons, big-valve heads and a pair of 48IDA Weber carburetors. Power output proved to be 185bhp on the dyno.**
(Author)

The Coral Red 1959 sedan of club President, Bill Schwimmer, represents the ultimate statement of what modern-day California Look is all about. The car sports a flawless paintjob yet, unlike the majority of the 1970s cars, retains the factory trim and bumpers. The latter have been fitted with a pair of EMPI bumper guards, something that wouldn't have been seen on any early California Look cars. The treatment of the windows differs, too, with pop-out rear quarter windows, factory wind-wings (rather than the one-piece door glass, which was a feature of many cars 20 years ago) and chrome trim in the sealing rubbers.

The choice of wheels hasn't changed, Schwimmer's '59 sporting a much-prized set of highly polished BRMs equipped with Caldwell recapped slicks on the rear. These are the latter-day equivalent of the old Goodyear Blue Streaks - race tires that have been adapted for road use. They allow the car to remain street-legal yet bite like a racing slick when called into action. As a finishing touch to the exterior, an original Economotors licence plate frame is fitted to the decklid.

Inside the sedan, the upholstery is a modern interpretation of the traditional style set by Don Bradford all those years ago, with stock seats

Schwimmer's ragtop retains all the original factory chrome trim and has also been equipped with a set of EMPI bumper guards. The car features the factory wind-wings in preference to the more traditional one-piece door glass. (Author)

The interior of Schwimmer's sedan has a flavor of the old days with its stock seating retrimmed with tweed inserts. Instrumentation is by Autometer while the steering wheel is by Nardi. Full harnesses show the car means business. (Author)

Dave Mason, also of Der Kleiner Panzers III, owns this mean black 1962 sedan which runs 11-second quarter miles. The chosen wheels are once again polished BRMs and the bodywork still retains the factory chrome trim.
(Mike Key)

Mason's car gets its impressive performance from a 78mm x 94mm engine with dual 48IDA Webers, Engle FK-89 camshaft and big-valve heads. A Vertex magneto provides the spark. Power output is 184bhp (310bhp with nitrous!).
(Mike Key)

**Orange County International Raceway in 1976? No, Le Mans, 1993! In France, too, the California Look style is growing in popularity by the day, with cars being built along the lines of the original Lookers of days gone by.** (Author)

retrimmed in grey naugahyde with grey tweed inserts. A wood-rimmed Nardi steering wheel is featured alongside a full complement of Autometer race-style gauges. However, it is under the decklid that the '59 really betrays its heritage.

An 82mm Gene Berg crankshaft works in conjunction with a set of Carillo conrods and Cima 90.5mm cylinders to result in a capacity of 2110cc. Big-valve cylinder heads, dual 48IDA Webers and a merged, large diameter exhaust system complete the 185bhp package. Only the 8.6:1 compression ratio suggests that this motor was built in the '90s, when only unleaded fuel is readily available. However,

while this combination remains street drivable, it is sufficient to give Schwimmer's car 12-second potential on the quarter mile. The old school era of California Look may have gone but with cars like this the spirit lives on – and Schwimmer is not alone in his intention to uphold the VW honor on street and strip.

Dave Mason's black 1962 is a real throwback with its BRMs and monster engine, too. This car started life as the daily driver of a little old lady (yes, such cars do exist) but soon came to be transformed into one of the fastest street-legal VWs ever. The sedan is powered by a 78mm x 94mm (2.2-liter)

Once upon a time it would have been difficult to even give a Type 3 away, but by the early 1980s the model had gained a wider acceptance. One of the first to be given the Look in Europe was the author's 1776cc 1972 Fastback in 1987.
(VolksWorld)

engine equipped with dual 48IDA Webers, nitrous oxide injection, an Engle FK-89 camshaft (with serious drag race only specification), 44mm x 37.5mm big valve cylinder heads and a Vertex magneto.

Pushing out in the region of 184bhp in normal trim and a massive 310bhp with the aid of nitrous oxide, the engine has proved capable of propelling the innocuous VW down the drag strip in 11.48secs/121.1mph! Consider this: the best time set by *Inch Pincher II*, the most famous drag race Volkswagen of all time, was slower than that set by Dave Mason's street car today! Proof indeed, as if any was needed, of how far the VW performance scene has progressed in a little over 20 years.

Elsewhere in the world, California Look as a style has spread like wildfire, with countries as far apart as England, Australia, Japan, Sweden, France and Norway all playing host to a large number of cars built along traditional lines. In these countries the expression California Look has been shortened to Cal Look and, perhaps sadly, applied to virtually any Volkswagen which has been lowered and painted a bright color. Cal Look VWs have swept through the event scene, almost to the exclusion of full-custom Bugs and off-road style VWs, once the mainstay of customizing outside the USA.

However, today it is not only the Volkswagen Bug that has come under the scrutiny of the Cal Look enthusiast. In the 1990s virtually any body style has gained acceptance, including Type 2 vans and buses, Type 3 Fastbacks, Notchbacks and Squarebacks (but not the cumbersome Type 4s) - even Karmann Ghia and Beetle cabriolets. The basic design parameters are much the same for all, with lowered suspension and a high-quality paintjob being number one priorities. Only in the choice of wheels and engine do these latter-day Cal Lookers differ radically from their forebears.

Where once it was necessary to fit wheels from EMPI (BRMs, five-spokes or GT Spyders) or maybe Porsche (but only in their original, dull factory finish), today almost anything goes. Polished Porsche 911 rims are extremely popular as are late-model aluminum wheels from any number of modern automobiles. Adaptors, once frowned upon, are relatively commonplace, but many still choose to have the brake drums redrilled to accept a non-VW wheel fitment.

In recognition of the popularity of the original BRM wheel and of its scarcity, Flat 4 of Japan went so far as to have replicas of this highly-sought after

Who, back in 1975, would have believed that a Type 2 would be considered a California Look VW? Radically lowered suspension, single-color paintjob and a set of polished replica Porsche wheels give this van an Orange County look..
(Author)

You said low? Check the mudflaps! Straight-axle suspension kits allow a sedan transmission to be fitted into an early Type 2, thereby doing away with the troublesome reduction boxes that give the stock Type 2 such a high ride height.
(Author)

wheel cast. While not pleasing the purists, this has helped to ensure the continuance of the old school look. Cast from aluminum, as opposed to the more fragile and corrosion-plagued magnesium BRMs, Flat 4 wheels are becoming more commonplace as people seek to recreate the Der Kleiner Panzer style without the expense of having to purchase the originals.

As far as horsepower is concerned, the cost of gasoline and insurance has put a stop to traditional California Look street racers being seen on a regular basis. In many parts of Europe it is strictly speaking illegal to modify the engine in any shape or form,

although that rarely seems to stop the determined enthusiast! By far the majority of modern Cal Lookers run small displacement engines - maybe 1641 or 1776cc - with dual single-throat carburetors or small dual-chokes. Greater emphasis has been placed on reliability and good gas mileage as opposed to outright horsepower. However, for the dedicated followers of the California Look in its purist form, there is fortunately no shortage of high-quality performance equipment available for the VW today. EMPI and Deano Dyno-Soars have long gone, but Gene Berg, Scat and FAT Performance live on in the company of a hundred other

123

Only the licence plate tag gives the game away that this isn't a DKP car from 1970. Chromed EMPI Sprint Star wheels have become sought after by the followers of the early style of California Look. Note the famous DKP eagle decal.
(Stéphane Szantai)

Porsche wheels became popular once Keith Goss had shown the way back in 1976, but few people ever polished them to this degree! Robert Bontuyan's Karmann Ghia coupé looks particularly striking in its deep orange paint.
(Stéphane Szantai)

businesses, all keen to market their latest products aimed at increasing the power output of the flat-four engine. It is worthy of note that the majority of the specialist VW businesses are still located in Orange County, many being run by people who took an active part in the development of the California Look twenty or more years ago.

Product development continues apace. Several companies now design and manufacture aftermarket VW cylinder heads, crankcases, crankshafts and conrods to a very high standard. These have enabled normally-aspirated drag race cars to run regularly down into the mid nine-second bracket, while turbocharged sedans can run up to half a second quicker. The spin-offs for road use are numerous, with a greater range of high-quality, high-

Hector Bonilla's '67 also sports a set of rare BRM wheels. His sedan displays many traditional California Look traits, including the dechromed bodywork, single-color paint scheme, one-piece windows and a nose-down hot rod rake.
(Stéphane Szantai)

performance products than ever before being made available to the Volkswagen enthusiast of the 1990s. Companies such as Bugpack (Dee Engineering) and Johnny's Speed & Chrome have been a part of the VW performance industry for many years and continue to this day to offer everything the Volkswagen owner could wish for.

With the development work being carried out by companies such as Kawell Racing Engines (yes, the same Dave Kawell who proved that a Karmann Ghia does work as a race car!), turbocharging has been shown to be a reliable way of extracting horsepower from the flat-four motor. Turbocharged dragsters are now regularly knocking on the six-second door at speeds approaching 180mph – but it has taken some ten years since Kawell broke into the sevens to reach that barrier.

Drag racing is now an extremely expensive but highly sophisticated sport, with timing computers, intercoolers and nitrous oxide injection systems all playing their part in the 1990s. Just as Gene Berg,

Flat 4 of Japan recognized the potential for a quality replica of the famous - and very hard to find - EMPI-Speedwell BRM magnesium wheel. The result is a wheel that is hard to distinguish from an original, except to the trained eye.
(Author)

**Gary Berg, son of VW performance specialist, Gene, built this beautiful metallic blue '67. This 13-second car is now owned by Rick Zavala, a member of the original DKP and owner of the black '67 seen at the end of chapter 2.** (Stéphane Szantai)

**While cabriolets didn't get much of a look in back in the old days, in the '90s anything goes. The combination of polished replica EMPI 8-spoke wheels, low profile tires and mile-deep metallic blue paint make this a VW to envy.** (Author)

As a style, it has indeed come of age.

Look there was only one magazine – *Hot VWs* – to spread the word, today there are several, including *VW Trends* (USA), *VolksWorld* (UK), *Cal* (Japan), *Super VW* (France) and *VW Scene* (Germany). Between them, they have helped to tell the world about the growth of the California Look and inspired many people to follow the lead set by Greg Aronson, Ron Fleming and a host of others almost a quarter of a century ago. No longer is the Look solely a product of California.

Dean Lowry and Ron Fleming did all those years ago, drag racers like Jack Sacchette and Adam Wik have crossed the divide from racer to race car engineer. The future, as a result, looks very bright indeed.

As far as street cars go, VWs like Bill Schwimmer's and Dave Mason's prove beyond doubt that the scene is alive and well, if not as large as it once was. Events may no longer host 10,000 spectators like the Bug-Ins of old, but they still show that the enthusiasm for the Volkswagen remains. In Europe and Scandinavia, however, events such as Sweden's Bug Run, England's *VolksWorld* Summer Nationals and France's *Super VW* Nationals all continue to expand in size and popularity. With their show cars, swap meets and drag races, these new events capture the spirit of west coast America of 15 or 20 years ago. The major difference is the weather! Whereas at the height of the original California

Stéphane Szantai recreates the cover of the famous February 1975 issue of *Hot VWs*. Traffic laws get stricter by the day and soon we may not even be allowed to drive a lowered California Looker. But until then, let's have fun!
(Stéphane Szantai)

Art Gutierrez built a red hot 48IDA Weber carbureted motor for his '67 sedan. Note the slicks and the highly polished big-bore muffler tucked under the fender. Ron Fleming, of DKP I (blue shirt) looks suitably impressed with Art's pride and joy.
(Stéphane Szantai)